Effective Approaches to the TOEIC® L&R Test

[Revised Edition]

TOEIC® L&R テスト：スコアアップのための総合英語【改訂新版】

by

Kiyomi Tanaka　Yuri Wada　Satoru Sakaki　Asako Kaneko

NAN'UN-DO

Download Audio

音声ファイル
無料 DL
のご案内

このテキストの音声を無料で視聴（ストリーミング）・ダウンロードできます。自習用音声としてご活用ください。
以下のサイトにアクセスしてテキスト番号で検索してください。

https://nanun-do.com　テキスト番号［**512068**］

※ 無線 LAN（WiFi）に接続してのご利用を推奨いたします。

※ 音声ダウンロードは Zip ファイルでの提供になります。
お使いの機器によっては別途ソフトウェア（アプリケーション）の導入が必要となります。

Read by

Chris Koprowski（米）
Emma Howard（英）
Shizuka Anderson（加）
Ian Bell（豪）

※ Effective Approaches to the TOEIC L&R Test【Revised Edition】音声ダウンロードページは以下の QR コードからもご利用になれます。

Effective Approaches to the TOEIC® L&R Test

[Revised Edition]

by
Kiyomi Tanaka　Yuri Wada　Satoru Sakaki　Asako Kaneko

はしがき

本書初版が出版されて以来，幸い多くの大学で先生方，学生の皆さんにTOEIC 教材として受け入れていただきました。その間も企業が採用，昇進の基準として一定以上の TOEIC スコアを求める傾向はますます強くなっています。ビジネスコミュニケーション力の「物差し」として信頼を得た試験と言えるでしょう。実務の需要に応じる形で，2016 年，TOEIC Test はよりオーセンティック（実際的）なコミュニケーションを重視する TOEIC® L&R Test に変更されました。このリニューアルに伴い，本書もこのたび，新形式に準拠した改訂版を出す運びとなりました。

改訂版では初版のコンセプト「TOEIC スコアアップにつながる重要ポイントを絞りこみ，問題の解法を丁寧に解説したうえで練習問題を提供」を継承するとともに，TOEIC 新形式の問題と学習効果を上げるための工夫を加えています。

特徴は以下の通りです。

・重要ポイントを明確にし，例題と解説を詳しく掲載。
・練習問題は学んだポイントを活かして解ける問題を厳選。
・リスニングの英文スクリプトを空所補充問題形式で掲載。
・テキスト巻末に，各ユニットの重要語句（Words and Phrases）を掲載。

TOEIC の問題形式が一部変更されても，語彙，文法，リスニング，読解それぞれの力が土台となることは変わりません。本書に沿って学習することで，総合的な土台が固まるだけでなく，重要ポイントを外さない効率の良い試験対策となります。ユニット一つ一つを確実にこなし，スコアアップにつながることを願っています。

最後になりましたが，初版の企画と執筆に多大な貢献をされた故田中清美先生，このたびの改訂版作成のために様々な相談に応じご尽力いただいた南雲堂編集部の加藤敦氏，全ページにわたり丁寧な英文指導をしていただいた Christofer Bullsmith 先生に，この場をお借りして心より感謝申し上げます。

和田ゆり

本書の構成と使い方

本書は全 20 ユニットから成り，各ユニットにリスニング，リーディングを 1 ～ 2 パートずつ，バランス良く取り入れています。全パートを扱い総合力の向上を図っていますが，目標に応じてパートごと，文法項目ごとなど，的を絞って活用していただくこともできます。

[Words & Phrases]

各ユニットの例題や練習問題で使われている重要語句について，意味を選ぶ形式で巻末に掲載しています。語彙を予習しておきましょう。

[Listening Section: PART 1，PART 2，PART 3，PART 4]

Technical Point

Technical Point とは，このユニットでマスターしたい内容を簡潔に表現したものです。内容に応じた聞き方の「こつ」を示したものもありますので，例題に入る前に一読してください。

例題については，音声を聞いて答えを選んだ後，もう一度聞いてスクリプトの空所補充をします。完成したスクリプトの内容と解説を参考にして，解答を確認しましょう。

[Training for the TOEIC®L&R TEST]

実際の TOEIC と同じ形式の練習問題です。例題で学んだ Technical Point を使えばほとんど解ける問題を集めています。この練習問題でテクニックを定着させましょう。

[Partial Dictation]

練習問題のスクリプトを空所補充問題形式にして掲載しています。Dictation は集中力を養い，聞き取りの力を定着させる有効な方法のひとつです。繰り返し聞いてスクリプトを完成させ，内容を確認してください。

[Reading Section: PART 5，PART 6，PART 7]

Technical Point

Listening Section と同様に，例題に入る前に一読してください。

・PART 5，6 については，TOEIC 文法問題の出題傾向に沿って，解法テクニックの視点からまとめています。例題を解いてから解説を読み，解答を確認してください。類題を Quiz として掲載しているユニットもあります。

・PART 7 には例題はありませんが，広告文，手紙文，図表など各リーディングテキストの特徴にあわせた Technical Point をあげ，読み方を解説しています。練習問題を解く前に目を通してください。

[Training for the TOEIC L&R TEST]

練習問題は実際の TOEIC と同じ形式で，Technical Point を使って解けるように文法事項や内容を絞っています。この練習問題でテクニックを定着させましょう。

CONTENTS

Effective Approaches

to the

TOEIC® L&R Test

Unit 1

PART 1 物の位置と状態を聞きとる

PART 5 語幹を共有する名詞・動詞・形容詞・副詞

Listening Section Part 1 物の位置と状態を聞き取る

Technical Point

● 物がどの様な状態になっているのかを聞きとろう

例題 1 次の写真を最も適切に描写している英文を選びなさい。 2

Ⓐ Ⓑ Ⓒ Ⓓ

下線部に聞きとった語句を書きなさい。

(A) There are lots of ________________ on the shelves.

(B) The ________________ are lying on the floor.

(C) Many baseball ________________ are on display.

(D) Some customers are buying ________________.

物が写っている写真は,「何がどの様な状態になっているのか」がポイントです。名詞に注意しながら,聞きとりましょう。(A) cups と (C) caps など,似ている音に気をつけます。

● 時制は現在形とは限らない

例題 2 次の写真を最も適切に描写している英文を選びなさい。 3

Ⓐ Ⓑ Ⓒ Ⓓ

下線部に聞きとった語句を書きなさい。

(A) Cooks ________________________ some food in the kitchen.

(B) The dishes are ________________________ in the dishwasher.

(C) The ________________ are stacked on the table.

(D) The food has been ________________________ on the table.

物の状態を表す際には，現在時制だけが使われるとは限りません。現在進行形はもちろん，現在完了形や受動態になる場合もあります。しかし，時制がなんであれ，ポイントとなる「物」が「どの様な状態になっているのか」が重要なので，単語をしっかりと聞き取りましょう。ここでは，食べ物が既にテーブルに並べられているので，(D) が正解になります。set out とは「陳列する，並べる」という意味ですが，食べ物 food が主語なので受動態となっています。

Training for the TOEIC L&R Test

PART 1: Select the sentence that best describes what you see in each picture.

1. 4

Ⓐ Ⓑ Ⓒ Ⓓ

2. 5

Ⓐ Ⓑ Ⓒ Ⓓ

3.

6

Ⓐ Ⓑ Ⓒ Ⓓ

Partial Dictation

1. (A) There's a lamp ______________________ the bed.

(B) There's a suitcase ______________________ on the bed.

(C) There are ______________________ cushions on the bed.

(D) ______________________ pictures are hanging on the wall.

2. (A) Shoppers are ______________________ some dairy products.

(B) Some produce is ______________________.

(C) The table is stacked with ______________________.

(D) The boxes on the stand are ______________________.

3. (A) The desks are arranged in a ______________________.

(B) There's a ______________________ next to the blackboard.

(C) There's ______________________ in the room.

(D) The ______________________ board is filled with notices.

Reading Section　PART 5　語幹を共有する名詞・動詞・形容詞・副詞

Technical Point

● 品詞の選択は空所の前後に注目

例題（　　）の中から正しい形を選びなさい。

a) The government announced (addition / add / additional / additionally) sets of measures to improve the supply-demand balance in the economy.

b) We must (finalization / finalize / final / finally) the commission for our suppliers.

a) のように語幹を共有する名詞，動詞，形容詞，副詞の選択は（　　）の前後に注目して，入れられる品詞の選択の幅を狭めて適当なものを選ぶのがひとつの方法です。この場合，（　　）は複数名詞 sets を修飾していると考えられるので，形容詞か，形容詞的に用いられる過去分詞（不規則動詞以外は動詞の原形 + ed）か，現在分詞 (-ing) しか入りません。addition は名詞であり，add は動詞の原形であるため名詞 sets を修飾できず，additionally も副詞であるため名詞 sets を直接修飾できません。したがって適当なものは sets を修飾できる形容詞の additional ということになります。

b) の場合は（　　）が助動詞 must と名詞 the commission の間にある事に着目すればどのような品詞が入るかが分かります（動詞の原形が入ります）。このようにまず文中におけるその語の位置や役割，また，前後関係からどういう品詞が入るかを把握することはとても大切です。ただし，最後に空所に選択した語を当てはめたときに文全体の意味がとおるかどうかチェックしましょう。文意がとおればそれが正解です。

● 品詞と活用の適当な形の見きわめ方のヒント

1. 冠詞 a，an，the や代名詞（または名詞）の所有格 your，his，her，~'s，etc. がついていれば後には必ず名詞が来る。（ただし，形容詞がその間に入ることもある）
2. 動詞は助動詞の直後に来る。
3. -ful，-able，-less，-ive などの語尾を持つ語は大部分，形容詞である。
4. 前置詞 in，on，at，of，for，except，after，before，etc. の後ろの動詞は必ず V-ing の形となる。
5. 不定詞 to の直後の動詞は必ず原形。
6. 副詞は -ly の語尾を持つものが大部分で動詞，形容詞または他の副詞を修飾する。

[Quiz]（　　）の中から正しい形を選びなさい。

(1) When you give a speech, making a good first (impression / impress / impressive) on your audience is essential.

(2) Although this medicine is quite (safe / safety / safely), it is better not to give it to children.

(3) This old film is still very (popularity / popular / popularization) among young Japanese.

(4) Mr. Walter's presentation on his proposed project was very (success / successful / successfully).

Training for the TOEIC L&R Test

PART 5: Select the best answer to complete each sentence.

1. Bus operators are not permitted to deposit fares or give change, so please have the ------- fare ready before you board any bus in the city.

(A) exact
(B) exactly
(C) equal
(D) equally

2. In that country, frozen foods and refrigerated products are ------- delivered by food manufacturers directly to supermarkets and convenience stores.

(A) common
(B) commonly
(C) commonness
(D) commonality

3. Two years ago, scientists at the National Science Research Institute ------ new methods of shock absorption during earthquakes for reinforced concrete buildings.

(A) invested
(B) investment
(C) investigated
(D) investigation

4. This show, which features teams of dancers competing for a trophy, is the ------- pop-culture entertainment.

(A) ultimately
(B) ultimateness
(C) ultimate
(D) ultimatum

5. To make this dish, many ingredients and spices must be ------- imported from South Asia.

(A) special
(B) specialty
(C) specially
(D) specialized

---

1. Ⓐ Ⓑ Ⓒ Ⓓ **2.** Ⓐ Ⓑ Ⓒ Ⓓ **3.** Ⓐ Ⓑ Ⓒ Ⓓ **4.** Ⓐ Ⓑ Ⓒ Ⓓ **5.** Ⓐ Ⓑ Ⓒ Ⓓ

6. The Associated Students of Apple University will be holding ------- to choose next year's student representatives.

(A) elects
(B) electors
(C) electing
(D) elections

7. Most people today are aware that fast food isn't the best choice for ------- a healthy diet.

(A) maintenance
(B) maintain
(C) maintainable
(D) maintaining

8. The driver asked passengers to push the stop request button to ------- when they wanted to get off the bus.

(A) signal
(B) sign
(C) signaling
(D) be signaled

9. The United States will have difficulty ------- effective sanctions through the Security Council.

(A) to pass
(B) pass
(C) passing
(D) for passing

10. The ------- between chronic depression and fatal heart attacks is not as well known as it should be.

(A) link up
(B) linked
(C) linking
(D) link

6. Ⓐ Ⓑ Ⓒ Ⓓ **7.** Ⓐ Ⓑ Ⓒ Ⓓ **8.** Ⓐ Ⓑ Ⓒ Ⓓ **9.** Ⓐ Ⓑ Ⓒ Ⓓ **10.** Ⓐ Ⓑ Ⓒ Ⓓ

Unit 2

PART 2 基本的な疑問文に応える

PART 6 気をつけるべき英語の語順

PART 7 広告文

Listening Section　PART 2　基本的な疑問文に応える

Technical Point

● 疑問文の応答は，形式よりも「意味」に注目する

例題 1　問いかけの文に対し応答として最も適切な英文を選びなさい。
下線部に聞きとった語句を書きなさい。　7

Do you remember when you saw him last?

(A) No, ________________ didn't.

(B) Yes, I ________________.

(C) ________________________, actually, at his apartment.　Ⓐ Ⓑ Ⓒ

最も基本的な疑問文として，Do you ...? や Are you ...? で始まる疑問文があります。これらは，Yes/No で答えることができるので，Yes/No 疑問文とよばれています。しかし，TOEIC では多くの場合，形が Yes/No 疑問文であっても，その答えに Yes/No などの語が含まれていないので注意しましょう。形を気にするよりも意味を聞きとることが大事です。

例題 2　問いかけの文に対し応答として最も適切な英文を選びなさい。
下線部に聞きとった語句を書きなさい。　8

Would you ________________ giving me a lift?

(A) No, please do not move it.

(B) Yes, go ahead and lift it up.

(C) ________________________. Where do you live?　Ⓐ Ⓑ Ⓒ

Training for the TOEIC L&R Test

PART 2: You will hear four questions and three possible responses to each. Select the best response to each question.

1. Ⓐ Ⓑ Ⓒ **2.** Ⓐ Ⓑ Ⓒ 9-12

3. Ⓐ Ⓑ Ⓒ **4.** Ⓐ Ⓑ Ⓒ

Partial Dictation

1. Are tickets for tonight's concert still ________________?

(A) Yes, the concert is tonight.

(B) The line forms over there.

(C) I'm ________________ they are all sold out.

2. Have you ________________ heard the news?

(A) The magazines are on the rack.

(B) ________________________ are you talking about?

(C) I'm sorry, but I'm afraid I can't.

3. Did you ________________ his presentation?

(A) I thought it was ________________.

(B) He's not my ________________.

(C) Yes, it was a nice ________________.

4. ________________________ like some help with your baggage?

(A) I would like this bag, please.

(B) Thanks, but I can ________________.

(C) No, it's too ________________.

Technical Point

● 英語は日本語と違って語順が大切

例題 (　　) の中の語句を入れる位置を / で示しなさい。

a) She is old to understand it. (enough)

b) He goes to the park. (often)

c) Tom put on. (it)

d) No help she get in completing the report on time. (did)

e) Were too low, she would not accept the position. (the pay)

a) 副詞は動詞を修飾する場合を除いてその修飾する語（句）の直前に置きますが，a) の enough や alone は例外でその修飾する語の直後におきます。

b) のように頻度（always，often，usually など）や否定（seldom，never，hardly，scarcely など）を表す副詞は通常，助動詞，be 動詞の直後，動詞の直前におきます。

c)「動詞 + 副詞」が代名詞 her，him，it などを目的語にする場合は代名詞をその間に入れます。例：turn it off.

d) の No help のような否定語（他に No sooner，Never，Little，Rarely など）が強調のために文頭におかれた場合には，その後の語順は疑問文とまったく同じです。否定語以外の語が強められるとS + VがV + S になることが多いようです。例：Up came the sun.

e) 仮定法の if のある文の最初の動詞 were，V-ed など，または助動詞 should，had などを文頭に持ってくれば if は省略されます。その場合，残った語の順序はそのままです。

[Quiz] (　　) の中の語句を入れる位置を / で示しなさい。

(1) Rarely I gotten sick in my life. (have)

(2) Jim promised to come late to school. (not)

(3) On this new sales system the future of the company. (depends)

(4) Had received the promotion, I would have purchased a new car. (I)

● 文選択問題では，代名詞や代名詞を含む言い換え表現に注目

選択肢の文中に it「それ」や these items「これらの商品」など，代名詞を含む表現ある場合は，空所の前に it が示す名詞や，these が示す複数の商品があるはずです。つまり選択肢の中で代名詞を含む文を入れてみて，その代名詞が示すものが空所の前にあれば正解の根拠となります。照合しながら「文選択問題」を解いてみましょう。

Training for the TOEIC L&R Test

PART 6: Select the best answers to complete the text.
Questions 1-4 refer to the following advertisement.

Enjoy your flight with Miracle Collar

"If you sleep sitting up during a flight, good head and neck support is essential." -------(1.) Dr. Richard Brown, a leading spinal surgeon who developed the new inflatable pillow. -------(2.) be a traveler who struggles to sleep while sitting up, give our patented, easy-to-inflate Miracle Collar a try. -------(3.) When you don't need it, it -------(4.) to stow in its pocket-sized pouch. Available in Size S (neck size to 14"), M (14 1/2 to 161/2"), or L (17" and over).

1. (A) Says so
(B) So says
(C) So does
(D) So did

Ⓐ Ⓑ Ⓒ Ⓓ

2. (A) If you
(B) Whether you
(C) Were you
(D) Should you

Ⓐ Ⓑ Ⓒ Ⓓ

3. (A) You should take a mild sleeping pill during a flight.
(B) You can release the stress from your body by doing that exercise.
(C) This innovative new product allows you a good sleep when you need it most.
(D) This is the most effective way to be relaxed.

Ⓐ Ⓑ Ⓒ Ⓓ

4. (A) becomes enough small
(B) becomes small enough
(C) enough becomes small
(D) small enough becomes

Ⓐ Ⓑ Ⓒ Ⓓ

Technical Point

● 広告文ではタイトルを確認し，商品の目的，特徴，対象などに注目する

広告文には，広告主が一般の人やユーザーに知ってもらいたい新しい商品やサービスなどの情報が掲載されています。したがって，その商品が何であるか，何のためのものか，どのような特徴があるか，また誰をターゲットにしているかを文中から把握することが大切です。TOEIC に出される広告文は新聞，雑誌などで目にする広告文とよく似ていますので，上の 4 点について自分自身に質問しながらそれらを読む練習をするのも良い方法です。時間に制限のある TOEIC の読解では，まずはタイトルに着目し，次に本文と設問の中のキーワードをスキャン（走り読み）し，最後に設問を見ながらもう一度，正答を探すために本文を検索していくというやり方が 1 つの方法です。

Training for the TOEIC L&R Test

PART 7: Select the best answer to each question.
Questions 1-2 refer to the following advertisement.

An investment I'm proud of

I'm proud of how beautiful my deck looks, and I'm really proud of the great value I got on Columbus Moonlight stains. Great protection, great value. Premium Moonlight stains bring out the wood's natural beauty and protect it from the harshest elements. I've always trusted my Columbus retailer's expert advice. And, whether I do the staining myself or have someone do it for me, it's an investment I'm proud of.

Columbus Stains
We make it simple to protect your home.
Call 222-555-9898, ext. 241 for a retailer near you.

1. What sort of products does Columbus Stains sell?
(A) Fabrics
(B) Deck furniture
(C) Wood finishes
(D) Stainless tableware
Ⓐ Ⓑ Ⓒ Ⓓ

2. What can be said about Premium Moonlight stains?
(A) They protect the wood.
(B) They are used indoors.
(C) They cover the wood completely.
(D) They are very expensive.
Ⓐ Ⓑ Ⓒ Ⓓ

Questions 3-5 refer to the following advertisement.

Summer School Program
July-August

Once again, we are proud to offer our popular summer session education programs appropriate for all grade levels. Weekly programs include family activities as well as academic courses that are standards-aligned and specially created by the Melon City Board of Education and other curriculum experts. Sign up now and receive daily newspapers and curriculum guides.

Application Form

Yes, please consider my class for: ____________________

SUMMER PROGRAM (5 days per week) DATE: FROM ________ TO ________

Summer School Name ____________________

Summer School Teacher's Name ____________________

Teacher's Phone ____________ Fax ____________ E-mail ____________

Grades & Subjects Taught ____________________

Teacher's Regular School Address ____________________

Fax coupon to: 476-555-5461
The Teacher's News—Education Department Summer Program
125 Cherry St., Melon City, NJ 09211- 2758

3. How long is each program?
(A) It varies.
(B) It lasts all summer.
(C) It is one week long.
(D) It is five days long.
Ⓐ Ⓑ Ⓒ Ⓓ

4. Who is the advertisement aimed at?
(A) Curriculum experts
(B) Primary school students
(C) Primary school teachers
(D) Parents
Ⓐ Ⓑ Ⓒ Ⓓ

5. Who is this summer school mainly for?
(A) Curriculum experts
(B) Students of all grade levels
(C) School teachers of all grade levels
(D) Parents
Ⓐ Ⓑ Ⓒ Ⓓ

Unit 3

PART 3 電話での会話

PART 5 数にからんだ語の用法①

Listening Section　PART 3　電話での会話

Technical Point

● 電話での会話は「用件」とそれに対する答えを的確に聞きとることが大切

TOEIC では短い時間で素早く状況を把握することが要求されるので，会話の音声が始まる前に受け答えのカギになる質問文に目を通しておいたほうがいいでしょう。

例題 会話を聞き，それに関する質問に対して最も適切なものを選びなさい。 13

1. How long will it take the woman to get to the coffee shop?

(A) At 3:10
(B) At 1:30
(C) Half an hour
(D) Thirteen minutes　Ⓐ Ⓑ Ⓒ Ⓓ

2. What is the most probable relationship between the speakers?

(A) Employer and employee
(B) Teacher and student
(C) Salesperson and customer
(D) Friends　Ⓐ Ⓑ Ⓒ Ⓓ

最初の問題のように時間を問う問題はほとんど when，how often，how many days，how long などで始まります。例題のように問題文に疑問詞がある場合，その疑問詞を正確に把握し，対応する答えを聞きとっていきます。また，話し手の関係に関する質問はほとんど who か what で始まります。選択肢を見て，選択肢に関連のある言葉が音声にあるかを聞きとります。もう一度会話を聞き，文を完成させてみましょう。

M: Hi, Nancy, this is Tom. Do you have time to talk?
W: Hi, Tom, sure. I was just 1._________________. What's up?
M: Well, I just finished taking 2.________________________ yesterday and I 3.____________________________________right now. I'm so bored. Would you like to get some coffee at Tully's with me?
W: Sure, that 4.________________________. I'll be there in thirty minutes.

Training for the TOEIC L&R Test

PART 3: You will hear two short conversations. Select the best answer to each question.

14

1. What kind of job is the woman applying for?
(A) Computer engineer
(B) Computer programmer
(C) Computer salesperson
(D) Computer repairperson
Ⓐ Ⓑ Ⓒ Ⓓ

2. What does the man ask the woman about?
(A) Her personality
(B) Her experience
(C) Her attitude
(D) Her age
Ⓐ Ⓑ Ⓒ Ⓓ

3. When does the man want to interview the woman?
(A) Today
(B) Next Monday
(C) Next Tuesday
(D) Next Wednesday
Ⓐ Ⓑ Ⓒ Ⓓ

15

4. When will the man make his presentation?
(A) Today
(B) Tomorrow
(C) The day after tomorrow
(D) Next week
Ⓐ Ⓑ Ⓒ Ⓓ

5. What is the most probable relationship between the speakers?
(A) Employer and employee
(B) Lawyer and client
(C) Colleagues
(D) Salesperson and customer
Ⓐ Ⓑ Ⓒ Ⓓ

6. Why can't the woman help the man?
(A) She is out of the office.
(B) She missed the deadline.
(C) She has her own project to finish.
(D) She is feeling too stressed out.
Ⓐ Ⓑ Ⓒ Ⓓ

Partial Dictation

Questions 1-3

W: I saw 1.__________ in the newspaper for 2.______________________________. I'm interested in applying 3.__________________.

M: Do you have 4.____________________ in the field?

W: Yes, I've worked in computer programming for over 5.________________________ now.

M: I see. Then, could you come in 6.__________________________ at three p.m. 7.__________________________?

W: Yes, of course, thank you.

Questions 4-6

W: Hi, Jack, this is Mary. Just thought I'd call to see how 1.______________________.

M: I'm really busy. I have to give a presentation on our new 2.____________________ ____________________ tomorrow and I'm not even 3.______________________.

W: You must be feeling pretty 4.____________________.

M: I sure am. Say, I'd really appreciate it if you could 5.__________________________ ____________________ and 6.__________________________.

W: I would, but I'm afraid I can't. Remember, I'm working on a 7.____________________________________ right now. The deadline is coming up very soon.

Reading Section　PART 5 数にからんだ語の用法 ①

Technical Point

● 主語と述語の関係を考え，単数扱いか複数扱いかを判断する

例題 1（　　）の中から正しい形を選びなさい。

a) Statistics (deal / deals) with numbers that represent facts or figures.

b) He comes from a family that (date / dates) back to the Middle Ages.

c) My family (is / are) all soccer fans, so we always go to the stadium together.

d) The old wooden furniture (were / was) preserved in excellent condition.

a) 学問を表す語は，最後に -s がついても，単数として扱います。
例：economics（経済学）, mathematics（数学）, linguistics（言語学）, statistics（統計学）など。

b) や c) のような集合名詞に関しては，集合名詞を「1 つのかたまり」として扱う場合は単数扱い (b) です。「かたまり」の中の「個々の構成員」に注目する場合は複数扱い (c) です。集合名詞には，他に class，audience（聴衆）などがあります。

d) のような不可算名詞は単数形で受けます。注意すべき不可算名詞は furniture，baggage，luggage，soap，chalk，paper，information，news などです。ただし，pieces of，sets of などが前につく場合は複数として扱います 。

● 主語が何かを見抜く

例題 2（　　）の中から正しい形を選びなさい。

a) The news release says that relations between management and workers in the company (is / are) getting better.

b) The old woman living next door to me always (irritate / irritates) me by making a lot of noise in the middle of the night.

c) There (is / are) not enough information to make a firm decision yet.

複雑な文章になってくると，主語が何なのかが分かりにくくなります。

a) では，that 節の中の主語が何かを見抜く必要があります。主語は relations ですが，between management and workers in the company という修飾部分があるために，分かりくい文章となっています。

b) も主語の old woman に living ... の修飾部分がついていますが，主語は単数 the old woman ですので，述語動詞には 3 単現の -s がつきます。

c) は主語が information という不可算名詞なので，単数形で受けます。

PART 5: Select the best answer to complete each sentence.

1. Every night, the audience ------- the actors a standing ovation.

(A) giving
(B) had gave
(C) gives
(D) give

2. Most people know that linguistics ------- something to do with languages.

(A) are
(B) be
(C) have
(D) has

3. He seemed to be surprised to learn that my family all ------- jobs related to accounting.

(A) has
(B) have
(C) does
(D) working

4. What the marketing manager is trying to say is that he believes sales of the new product will increase as time ------- by.

(A) go
(B) goes
(C) pass
(D) passed

5. The new sales manuals which are supposed to be distributed to all store managers by now ------- not arrived yet.

(A) have
(B) has
(C) were
(D) are

1. Ⓐ Ⓑ Ⓒ Ⓓ **2.** Ⓐ Ⓑ Ⓒ Ⓓ **3.** Ⓐ Ⓑ Ⓒ Ⓓ **4.** Ⓐ Ⓑ Ⓒ Ⓓ **5.** Ⓐ Ⓑ Ⓒ Ⓓ

6. A great deal of change ------- been seen in the automotive industry in recent years.

(A) is
(B) are
(C) have
(D) has

7. There is no indication of how much baggage ------- unloaded.

(A) were
(B) was
(C) be
(D) done

8. The number of people who are unemployed ------- been increasing.

(A) have
(B) has
(C) are
(D) is

9. Each generation ------- to be able to tolerate the noises it grows up with and to despise the additional noises that appear later.

(A) seem
(B) seems
(C) looks like
(D) look

10. If there ------- enough time to finish the report today, finish it at home tonight.

(A) was not
(B) are not
(C) is not
(D) has not

6. Ⓐ Ⓑ Ⓒ Ⓓ **7.** Ⓐ Ⓑ Ⓒ Ⓓ **8.** Ⓐ Ⓑ Ⓒ Ⓓ **9.** Ⓐ Ⓑ Ⓒ Ⓓ **10.** Ⓐ Ⓑ Ⓒ Ⓓ

Unit 4

PART 4 スピーチ

PART 6 数にからんだ語の用法②

PART 7 チャットのやりとり

Listening Section　PART 4 スピーチ

Technical Point

● スピーチの聞きとりではその状況を素早く想定することが大事

スピーチは相互に交わされる通常の会話文と違い，大勢の人々に対して 1 人の人がする演説です。この場合も，スピーチの音声が始まる前に状況を把握するヒントとなる設問と選択肢をさっと見ておいたほうがいいでしょう。

例題 スピーチを聞き，それに関する質問に対して最も適切なものを選びなさい。 16

1. What does the woman think of Sam?

(A) He is brave.
(B) He is jealous.
(C) He is patient.
(D) He is considerate.

Ⓐ Ⓑ Ⓒ Ⓓ

2. When did Sam and the speaker get married?

(A) Fifteen years ago
(B) Fifty years ago
(C) For fifteen years
(D) For fifty years

Ⓐ Ⓑ Ⓒ Ⓓ

最初の 2，3 文でどのような人が何のためにスピーチをしようとしているかが分かります。最初の問題のように意見を問う問題では選択肢を見ながらヒントとなる単語や句を捉えていきます。また，選択肢を見た時に 2 番目の問題のような数字を選ばせる問題がある時は数字を正確に聞きとり記憶することが重要です。もう一度聞き，スピーチを完成させてみましょう。

Thank you for coming to our 1.________________ wedding anniversary party this evening. We came to this community twenty-eight years ago with our lovely children, Alex, Betty, and Larry, right over there, and have loved every day of our life here. 2.________________ my husband, who has been a 3.________________ to our children. I 4.________________ his sophistication, his terrific sense of humor, and his 5.________________ for others. After 6.________________ together, I think I love Sam even more today than I did on the day we got married. I can only say how grateful I am to Sam for a great life together. Thank you very much.

Training for the TOEIC L&R Test

PART 4: You will hear two short talks. Select the best answer to each question.

17

1. Who most likely is the speaker?
(A) A secretary
(B) A professor
(C) A customer
(D) A company president
Ⓐ Ⓑ Ⓒ Ⓓ

2. How does the speaker feel?
(A) Determined
(B) Discouraged
(C) Dependable
(D) Demanding
Ⓐ Ⓑ Ⓒ Ⓓ

3. What changes are taking place in the company?
(A) It will separate into different parts.
(B) It will have a new organization.
(C) The workers will build a new bridge.
(D) It is looking for new natural resources.
Ⓐ Ⓑ Ⓒ Ⓓ

18

4. What is the main purpose of the speech?
(A) To announce a new meeting schedule
(B) To introduce the guest speaker
(C) To explain the nation's economic condition
(D) To give advice to the attendees
Ⓐ Ⓑ Ⓒ Ⓓ

5. Who is the guest speaker?
(A) A physician
(B) A novelist
(C) An economist
(D) An architect
Ⓐ Ⓑ Ⓒ Ⓓ

6. What will take place next?
(A) Attendees will ask questions.
(B) The dean will give a short introduction.
(C) The guest speaker will give his speech.
(D) The guest speaker will leave for another appointment.
Ⓐ Ⓑ Ⓒ Ⓓ

Partial Dictation

Questions 1-3

Good afternoon, everyone. Thanks for joining this meeting. Last April we 1.__________ __________ for the new year. Everything we do from now on is about 2.__________ __________________ that blueprint. Today, in this meeting, we will be announcing a 3.__________________ the company that brings 4.____________________ of the company together to create a stronger bridge between our customers and us. We live in a world of ever-more 5.________________________ and ever-greater 6.____________. We can only succeed in this world if we can 7.__________________ __________ the resources to offer great new services and 8.______________ __________ to our customers.

Questions 4-6

Good morning. I'm Eric Ross, Assistant Dean at Quebec University. 1.______________ __________ our Dean, James Block, who unfortunately could not be with us today, I want to welcome all of you here as part of our distinguished 2.______________. I have the honor and the privilege of 3.______________________ today our guest speaker, Dr. Donald Parker, one of the most 4.____________________ in Canada. He will speak to us today on pressing 5.____________________ before the nation. After his talk, Professor Parker will 6.________________________ for a limited period of time only because he has to leave for a 7.__________________________ appointment.

Reading Section　PART 6 数にからんだ語の用法 ②

Technical Point

● 要注意の決まりごとを覚えよう

例題（　　）の中から正しい形を選びなさい。

a) A number of people (was / were) standing at the gate when the King came out.

b) The number of schools in this district (has / have) greatly increased.

c) Every student (has / have) to submit the essay by April 3rd.

d) The teacher as well as the students (seems / seem) to be very tired.

e) Not only John but also you (is / are) responsible for implementing this project.

f) Either he or I (is/ am) to try to convince the CEO to approve our marketing plans.

g) Twenty years (is / are) the usual time required to pay back a home loan.

主語となる名詞に様々な修飾語がついて，動詞の形が制約されることがあります。決まりごとですので，しっかり覚えましょう。

・a number of ~　「たくさんの～」　→ 複数扱い
　(cf.) the number of ~　「～の数」　→ 単数扱い

・each, every, everything, something など → 単数扱い

・A as well as B「B と同様に A も」= Not only B but (also) A「B だけでなく A も」
　→ 動詞は両方とも A に一致します (書き換えた時 A，B の位置が変わるので注意)。

・(Either) A or B「A か B かどちらか」→ 動詞に近いほうに動詞が一致します。つまり平叙文では B に，疑問文では A に一致します。例：Are you or he responsible for it?

・時間，距離，量などの表現がまとまった単位を表す時は，形は複数形でも単数の動詞で受けます（例題 g)。ただし，時の経過をいうときの years，months，days，hours は複数に扱われます。
　例：Five years have passed since he left school.

PART 6: Select the best answers to complete the text.
Questions 1-4 refer to the following university course bulletin.

Sociology 200
Mark A. Smith

Sociological Principles and Problems

This course ------- **1.** students to characteristic modes of sociological analysis. Rather than surveying the discipline, it reviews empirical work to provide insight into how sociologists explain phenomena like conflict, inequality, and deviant behavior. ------- **2.** Each student ------- **3.** expected to work with primary texts and comment critically on lectures and readings. Active participation in discussions as well as three critical essays on listed books ------- **4.** required.

1. (A) be introduced
(B) introducing
(C) introduces
(D) introduce

Ⓐ Ⓑ Ⓒ Ⓓ

2. (A) The key difference between sociology and anthropology is that the former concentrates on society while the latter focuses on culture.
(B) Our course pack is available at University Document Service.
(C) Essays should be 8-10 pages.
(D) Such input will help students understand the principles of sociology.

Ⓐ Ⓑ Ⓒ Ⓓ

3. (A) be
(B) are
(C) is
(D) should

Ⓐ Ⓑ Ⓒ Ⓓ

4. (A) be
(B) are
(C) is
(D) were

Ⓐ Ⓑ Ⓒ Ⓓ

Reading Section　PART 7 チャットのやりとり

Technical Point ● 書き手の意図を読み取る

text-message chain と呼ばれるチャットのやりとりでは，書き手の意図を読み取ることが大切です。カジュアルな表現が使用されることが多く，省略される語も少なくありません。文脈から書き手の意図を探りましょう。

Training for the TOEIC L&R Test

PART 7: Select the best answer to each question.
Questions 1 and 2 refer to the following text message chain.

Alana Olson (5:03 P.M.)
Do you mind if my husband joins us next week? His business meeting was canceled, and he's a big fan of Chopin.

Lily Poland (5:10 P.M.)
Of course not. I've already booked us four seats, so we're good to go.

Alana Olson (5:55 P.M.)
Thanks. Where shall we meet?

Lily Poland (6:20 P.M.)
How about in front of the venue? Too crowded?

Alana Olson (6:25 P.M.)
The theater has a big entrance. Shouldn't be a problem.
I'll text you when I arrive, anyway.

Lily Poland (6:30 P.M.)
Got it, see you then!

1. At 5:10 P.M., what does Ms. Poland mean by "we're good to go"?
(A) They are happy to go out together.
(B) They are good at playing Chopin.
(C) Ms. Poland has already bought the tickets for all of them, so Ms. Olson doesn't need to purchase the tickets.
(D) Ms. Poland feels good to go to the concert.　Ⓐ Ⓑ Ⓒ Ⓓ

2. Where will they meet?
(A) At the entrance of the theater.
(B) Beneath the theater.
(C) At the back of the hall.
(D) They haven't decided yet.　Ⓐ Ⓑ Ⓒ Ⓓ

Unit 5

PART 1 人物の動作と様子

PART 5 ねらわれやすい現在形と未来を表す表現

Listening Section　PART 1 人物の動作と様子

Technical Point

● 人物の動作や様子を聞きとる

例題 1 次の写真を最も適切に描写している英文を選びなさい。 19

Ⓐ Ⓑ Ⓒ Ⓓ

下線部に聞きとった語句を書きなさい。

(A) He is ________________ hands.

(B) He is ________________ a briefcase.

(C) He is ________________ a surfboard.

(D) He is ________________ a boat.

人物が写っている写真に関しては，その人物が何をしているか，何を身につけているか，などが聞かれることがあります。特に動詞部分に注意しましょう。

● 「着ている」のは服だけとは限らない

例題 2 次の写真を最も適切に描写している英文を選びなさい。 20

Ⓐ Ⓑ Ⓒ Ⓓ

下線部に聞きとった語句を書きなさい。

(A) The man is wearing ________________ eyewear.

(B) The man is ________________ a pair of glasses.

(C) The man is ________________.

(D) The man is putting on his ________________.

人物が身につけている物は，服（clothes や jacket，skirt，suit，dress など）の他にも帽子や眼鏡など，様々なものがあります。それら身につけるものを表す単語に十分に注意しましょう。

Training for the TOEIC L&R Test

PART 1: Select the sentence that best describes what you see in each picture.

1. 21

Ⓐ Ⓑ Ⓒ Ⓓ

2. 22

Ⓐ Ⓑ Ⓒ Ⓓ

3.

23

Ⓐ Ⓑ Ⓒ Ⓓ

Partial Dictation

1. (A) He's ______________________________ a picture.

(B) He's making a ______________________________.

(C) He's using an ______________________________.

(D) He's ______________________________ in line.

2. (A) He's ______________________________ a chair.

(B) He's ______________________________ in the kitchen.

(C) He's ______________________________ in front of his car.

(D) He's ______________________________ outside.

3. (A) She's holding a ______________________________.

(B) She's relaxing ______________________________.

(C) She's ______________________________ some wine.

(D) She's ______________________________ the wall.

Reading Section　PART 5 ねらわれやすい現在形と未来を表す表現

Technical Point

● 時・条件を表す副詞節では現在形を選ぶ

例題 1（　　）の中から正しい形を選びなさい。

a) The earth (go / goes / will go / went) around the sun.

b) We will wait at the station until the client (come / comes / will come / came).

c) We will go on a field trip if it (be / is / will be / was) sunny tomorrow.

a) の文全体の内容を推測すると,「地球は太陽の周りを回っている」です。このように「現在の事実」「いつも（普段）そうである」といった内容を述べる時，英語では現在形を用います。

b) で最も伝えたい内容 (＝主節) は "We will wait at the station" です。until 以降は副詞節と呼ばれます。「副詞節」とは，仮にその部分を文から削除しても文の意味が通るものです。主節は文の根幹であるため削除すると意味が通らなくなります。b) では "until ～"(副詞節) を削除しても "We will wait at the station"(主節) で十分意味が通ります。さて，解答の導き方ですが，最も重要な「主節」で will が使われているため「未来の話」であることは聞き手に伝わります。そのため重要度の下がる副詞節では will を再度使わずに,「実際にあること」と考えて現在形を用います。このように副詞節内では未来を表す内容でも現在形（「完了」を強調したいときは現在完了形）を用います。

c) も，b) と同様に主節 "We ～ a field trip" で will が使われているため，if 以降の副詞節内の動詞は現在形で表します。"We ～ a field trip" が主節で if 以下が副詞節だというのは，"if ～ tomorrow" を削除しても "We will go on a field trip" で十分意味が通ることから分かります。

b) や c) のような「時・条件を表す副詞節」を導く接続詞には when, if, unless, till, until, by the time, whether, once, as soon as などがあります。主節に will があれば，これらの接続詞に続く副詞節内の動詞は現在形で表します。

● 覚えておくべき未来を表す表現　will do, be going to do, be about to do, be to do

例題 2（　　）の中から正しい形を選びなさい。

a) Mr. and Mrs. Shinozaki (will be / have been / was) back in one hour.

b) The train (was about to arrive / has arrived / arrives), so I rushed to the platform.

c) Our manager (arrived / has arrived / is to arrive) at the office at 9 tomorrow morning.

a) では，後半に "in one hour"「１時間後」とあるので，未来の表現である will を選びます。

b) では，"so ～ the platform" から「まさに do しようとする」という意味を表す "be about to do" が最も適切です。"be about to do" は "be going to do" よりも差し迫った未来を表します。

c) では，"tomorrow morning" から未来の内容だと分かります。"be to do" で「do することになっている」という義務・予定・運命・可能・意図を表します。頭文字を取って「ぎょうかいの "be to do"」と覚えましょう。

Training for the TOEIC L&R Test

PART 5: Select the best answer to complete each sentence.

1. We will agree to this contract if these conditions ------- met.

(A) are
(B) will be
(C) were
(D) had been

2. The conference ------- held at the trade center next month.

(A) is
(B) was
(C) is to be
(D) has been

3. If the weather ------- beautiful, we can see Mt. Rainier from this observation tower.

(A) will be
(B) is
(C) was
(D) has been

4. We'll have to wait until the shipment ------- in.

(A) come
(B) came
(C) comes
(D) will come

5. Please give me a ring on my mobile as soon as he ------- at the airport.

(A) arrive
(B) arrives
(C) arrived
(D) will arrive

1. Ⓐ Ⓑ Ⓒ Ⓓ **2.** Ⓐ Ⓑ Ⓒ Ⓓ **3.** Ⓐ Ⓑ Ⓒ Ⓓ **4.** Ⓐ Ⓑ Ⓒ Ⓓ **5.** Ⓐ Ⓑ Ⓒ Ⓓ

6. He says he will prepare some visual material for his presentation when he ------- back to the office.

(A) get
(B) got
(C) gets
(D) will get

7. The manager ------- the office when the president called him.

(A) was left
(B) has left
(C) is leaving
(D) was about to leave

8. I wonder if it ------- tomorrow.

(A) rain
(B) rains
(C) will rain
(D) would rain

9. Once you ------- a room, you will receive an e-mail confirming your reservation.

(A) booked
(B) will book
(C) would book
(D) have booked

10. By the time we ------- out the main cause of this problem, we had already suffered in the market to a great extent.

(A) find
(B) can find
(C) would find
(D) found

6. Ⓐ Ⓑ Ⓒ Ⓓ **7.** Ⓐ Ⓑ Ⓒ Ⓓ **8.** Ⓐ Ⓑ Ⓒ Ⓓ **9.** Ⓐ Ⓑ Ⓒ Ⓓ **10.** Ⓐ Ⓑ Ⓒ Ⓓ

Unit 6

PART 2 いろいろな Wh- 疑問文

PART 6 ねらわれやすい過去形と完了形の表現

PART 7 図表と文書

Listening Section　PART 2 いろいろな Wh- 疑問文

Technical Point

● PART 2 では，最初の語や表現に集中する

例題 1 問いかけの文に対し応答として最も適切な英文を選びなさい。
下線部に聞きとった語句を書きなさい。　24

_________________ are you going to London on your business trip?

(A) _________________, I am.

(B) _________________ week.

(C) By _________________.　Ⓐ Ⓑ Ⓒ

PART 2 では例題 1 のような Wh- 疑問文の出題が多く見られます。そのため PART 2 では，特に発話の最初の表現に集中し，「問われていることは何か」をつかめば，正答が導けます。“5W1H (Who / Which / What / Where / When / How) + Why” は多くの人にとって聞き慣れた表現であるため，比較的聞き取りやすいと思います。

例題 2 問いかけの文に対し応答として最も適切な英文を選びなさい。
下線部に聞きとった語句を書きなさい。　25

_________________ is the daytime temperature in Tokyo in December?

(A) It’s much colder _____________________.

(B) December is the _______________ of the year.

(C) It’s usually between _____________________ degrees Celsius.　Ⓐ Ⓑ Ⓒ

who，where，when などの疑問詞と違い what で始まる疑問文は疑問詞を聞いただけでは選択肢の幅を絞込むのは難しいかもしれません。what に続く be 動詞 / 助動詞，それらの時制，主語が何かに気をつけます。what で問われるのは名前，職業，関係，言動，感情，考えなど人に関する事柄や出来事，事実，予定など幅広いものがあります。また慣用語句で問われる場合もあります。What’s for 食事名？「食事は何にするの？」What about ~？「～はどう？」What time do you have?「何時ですか。」などです。またすべての疑問詞に言えることですが，when に対する時間の答えといった典型的な型のほか，例えば What time do you have? に対して I’m sorry，I don’t have a watch. などが答えになる変化球もありますので気をつけましょう。

Training for the TOEIC L&R Test

PART 2: You will hear four questions and three possible responses to each. Select the best response to each question.

1. (A) (B) (C) **2.** (A) (B) (C) 26-29

3. (A) (B) (C) **4.** (A) (B) (C)

Partial Dictation

1. ________________ was Mr. Gale's plan to increase our sales?

(A) He says we need to ________________ our products better.

(B) The sale ________________ next Friday.

(C) Yes, ________________ sales is not easy.

2. ________________ is coming with us?

(A) No. I wouldn't ________________ going.

(B) Jack and Bob, and Jill ________________ come, too.

(C) Mary ________________ last time.

3. ________________________ are you leaving for the airport?

(A) By ________________ is the fastest.

(B) I think it takes nearly ________________________.

(C) I plan to leave here at about ________________.

4. ________________ have you been?

(A) I ________________ to go to Hawaii someday.

(B) ________________, to get some stationery.

(C) You can buy ________________ at the corner market.

Technical Point

● last ～ , ～ ago, yesterday といった過去の一時点を表す表現があれば現在完了形は×

例題 1（　　）の中から正しい形を選びなさい。

a) He (receive / receives /received / has received) his MBA from the university last year.

b) The reform plan (is / was / has been / will be) announced three years ago.

c) He (establishes / established / has established / will establish) this company in 1973.

現在完了形は「現在と繋がりのある内容」を表すため，過去の一時点を表す表現と共に使うことができません。a) ～ c) には全て「過去の一時点を表す表現」（下線部）があるため，現在完了形は選べません。それぞれ文の内容が過去ですので，全て過去形が正解となります。

TOEIC で狙われる「過去の一時点を表す表現」には，次のようなものがあります。文中にこれらの表現があれば，過去形（内容によっては過去完了形）を選びましょう。

last month，three weeks ago，yesterday，in 1973，when he was there など。

● since ～ , for ～ , over ～ , recently, lately 等 , 現在と繋がりがある語句は現在完了形と共に使う

過去に起きた出来事が「現在と関係がある」と話し手が考えている場合, 現在完了形 “have ＋ 過去分詞” で表します。感覚的にはあくまでも「現在」です。主に「現在と繋がりのある」表現 since ～「～以来」，for ～「～のあいだ」，over ～「～に渡って」，recently，lately「最近」等と共に用います。なお since があれば last や ago があっても完了形を用いるので注意してください。

例題 2（　　）の中から正しい形を選びなさい。

a) Lately our business (stagnate / has stagnated / had stagnated / will stagnate) due to the long-term recession.

b) The unemployment rate (is rising / was rising / has risen / rose) since last year.

a) では “lately”「最近」，b) では “since ～ ”「～以来（今まで）」という現在と繋がりのある語が文中にあることから，a)，b) ともに現在完了形の “have (has) ＋ 過去分詞 ” を選びます。

Training for the TOEIC L&R Test

PART 6: Select the best answers to complete the text.
Questions 1-4 refer to the following advertisement.

14th of February

Excerpt from the Annual Report

The Annual Report has found two areas where errors ------- **1.** made in the administration of the medical insurance scheme over a number of months. This has affected a significant number of people receiving the benefits. The Report found that:

- Payments ------- **2.** adjusted incorrectly since April last year.
- Some applications have been assessed using incorrect criteria.

The scheme administrators ------- **3.** the individuals affected in emails sent on the 1st of February and are now working on individual cases. The bulk of these cases will be resolved. ------- **4.**

1. (A) have
(B) have been
(C) was
(D) would be

2. (A) are
(B) were
(C) will be
(D) have been

3. (A) notify
(B) have notified
(C) notified
(D) will notify

4. (A) Claimants will be reimbursed by the end of March.
(B) We hope claimants will visit a hospital by the end of February.
(C) All the claimants are advised to void this notice.
(D) Only a few claimants were affected as far as we know.

1. Ⓐ Ⓑ Ⓒ Ⓓ　**2.** Ⓐ Ⓑ Ⓒ Ⓓ　**3.** Ⓐ Ⓑ Ⓒ Ⓓ　**4.** Ⓐ Ⓑ Ⓒ Ⓓ

Technical Point

● 図表と文書の問題では，図表のタイトルと文書のタイトルをチェック

図表と文書の問題で見落としがちなのが，タイトル（表題）です。タイトルを見れば何に関する図表・文書であるかを簡単に推測することができます。書き手は，読み手にわかりやすいようにタイトルをつけるからです。

タイトルを見て内容を推測した後は，他の TOEIC 長文対策と同様に設問を先にチェックします。図表の問題は情報が整理されているため，必要な情報を見つけやすいのが特徴です。先に設問をチェックして解答に要求される情報を短時間で見つけましょう。ただしこのタイプの問題では比較的簡単に解答できるため，思わぬミスをしてしまうこともあります。設問をよく読み，早とちりやケアレスミスに注意して下さい。

Training for the TOEIC L&R Test

PART 7: Select the best answer to each question.
Questions 1-5 refer to the following memo and chart.

Timetable of Meetings

Report by Head of the Administration

- The report proposes a timetable of meetings for the period October to March.
- Staff members are recommended to approve this timetable as soon as possible.

A report setting out a proposed timetable of meetings for the next two quarters has been released by members of the administration. This report sets out a draft timetable which is attached as an appendix.

In the draft timetable particular factors relating to each committee have been taken into account. The draft timetable has been circulated to current chairs and vice-chairs and their views have been reflected in preparing the new program.

The board of directors agreed that its annual meeting would be held in November. The meeting previously held in September is now no longer part of the timetable. Consequently, any possible clashes with other meetings are avoided.

Appendix **Proposed Timetable of Meetings**

Division	Day	Time	Oct	Nov	Dec	Jan	Feb	Mar
Public Relations	Wed	09:00	11	8	6	10	7	28
Marketing Strategy	Mon	14:00	16				12	
Shares	Fri	14:00			8			9
Operating Committee	Wed	14:00	18				7	
Board of Directors	Thurs	13:30		23		25		29

1. What are the memo and chart mainly about?
(A) Making sure that employees follow the schedule.
(B) Asking staff members to approve the timetable.
(C) Letting staff members know the length of each meeting.
(D) Ordering members to make up their schedules in advance.

2. Which meeting is to be held most often?
(A) Public Relations
(B) Marketing Strategy
(C) Shares
(D) Operating Committee

3. What process has this timetable gone through?
(A) It was created on a computer.
(B) It was developed by members of Public Relations.
(C) It was discussed in the annual meeting.
(D) It was checked by the company's executives.

4. What is NOT shown in the memo and chart?
(A) The time when each meeting begins.
(B) The name of the group holding each meeting.
(C) The agenda of the board of director's meeting held in September.
(D) The person responsible for this report.

5. What can be inferred from the memo and chart?
(A) This organization's share price is going down.
(B) There are more than five members in the Standing Committee.
(C) Operating Committee members have to choose one between two meetings.
(D) No meetings will clash with one another.

1. Ⓐ Ⓑ Ⓒ Ⓓ **2.** Ⓐ Ⓑ Ⓒ Ⓓ **3.** Ⓐ Ⓑ Ⓒ Ⓓ **4.** Ⓐ Ⓑ Ⓒ Ⓓ **5.** Ⓐ Ⓑ Ⓒ Ⓓ

Unit 7

PART 3 カジュアルな日常会話

PART 5 比較がらみの表現①

Listening Section　PART 3 カジュアルな日常会話

Technical Point

● あらかじめ設問に目を通し，キーワードを抜き出す

多くの会話は，カジュアルな日常会話から成っています。発話者の関係などに気を配りながら，設問で聞かれていることに注意し聞きとりましょう。会話は男女各 1 名ずつで構成されるものがほとんどですが，なかには 3 人による会話もあります。それぞれの役割に注意しましょう。

例題 会話を聞き，それに関する質問に対して最も適切なものを選びなさい。 30

How does the man feel about the main character?

(A) He respects her.

(B) He doesn't like her so much.

(C) He thinks that she is a boring person.

(D) She inspires him.

Ⓐ Ⓑ Ⓒ Ⓓ

男性が女性に貸していた本の内容に関する会話です。質問は「男性は本の主人公に関して，どの様に感じたか」です。男性が自分の意見を言う部分に注目し，空所を埋めながら会話を聞いてみましょう。

W: Here's the book I borrowed. Sorry for keeping it for such a long time.

M: No problem. So, 1.______________________________ it?

W: Well, the story was a little boring, but the main character was inspirational. I especially liked the way she talked.

M: Really? I found that rather 2.________________. She seemed awfully selfish to me.

男性と女性，どちらの話し手も主人公に対する感想を述べているので，男性はどう思ったのか，感情を表す形容詞などに注意しながら聞きとります。女性は，主人公を inspirational（知的に人を刺激するような人）として肯定的に受け取っていますが，男性は annoying（嫌な）と感じています。その後，男性が主人公を形容するのに使った selfish（身勝手）という形容詞も，男性の感情を表すヒントとなるでしょう。

Training for the TOEIC L&R Test

PART 3: You will hear two short conversations. Select the best answer to each question.

31

1. What are the speakers mainly talking about?
(A) Their plans for this evening
(B) The plan for a school trip
(C) Exhibition methods
(D) The trip they recently had
Ⓐ Ⓑ Ⓒ Ⓓ

2. What possible problem do they discuss?
(A) It is too expensive.
(B) It is not educational.
(C) It opens only on Wednesday morning.
(D) There might be too many visitors.
Ⓐ Ⓑ Ⓒ Ⓓ

3. What will they probably do next?
(A) Check the admission fee.
(B) Go to the museum.
(C) Study the interactive display method.
(D) Calculate the time.
Ⓐ Ⓑ Ⓒ Ⓓ

32

4. What is the man going to do?
(A) Take care of the woman's cat
(B) Go to his sister's wedding
(C) Take a trip to Scotland
(D) Ask Mrs. Lorenzo
Ⓐ Ⓑ Ⓒ Ⓓ

5. Why did the woman turn down the man's request?
(A) She is going to be away for a while.
(B) Her son has a problem with cats.
(C) She doesn't like cats.
(D) She's visiting her daughter.
Ⓐ Ⓑ Ⓒ Ⓓ

6. What surprised the woman?
(A) That Mrs. Lorenzo has a daughter
(B) That the man's sister is getting married
(C) That the man has a cat
(D) That Mrs. Lorenzo will go to Scotland
Ⓐ Ⓑ Ⓒ Ⓓ

Partial Dictation

Questions 1-3

W1: So does anyone have any suggestion for the place? It should be educational, of course, but most importantly, we want our 1.________________ to enjoy the trip.

M: How about the History Museum in Holly that has recently opened? I heard that it exhibits things in a very unique way. That is … um, interactive display.

W2: Yes, I heard about it too. But isn't it still too 2.________________ ? I worry if the students can take enough time to appreciate each object with so many people around.

M: They have some special time period allotted for school excursions. Let me check … it's Wednesday morning, from 9 to 12.

W1: That sounds perfect! Now, what about the 3.________________?

Questions 4-6

M: I'm leaving for New York tomorrow to attend my sister's 1.________________, and I have 2.________________ to ask of you. Could you take care of my cat while I am away?

W: I wish I could, but my son is 3.________________ to cats. Mrs. Lorenzo might be able to help you. She loves cats, you know.

M: She is on vacation. She is visiting her daughter in Scotland.

W: She has a daughter? I'm 4.________________ to hear that. She has never mentioned a daughter to me.

Reading Section　PART 5 比較がらみの表現 ①

Technical Point

● 基本的な 3 つのタイプの表現

例題 1（　）の中から正しい形を選びなさい。

a) Ms. Brown types (accurately as / as accurately as) Ms. Lee.

b) Rick seems to be feeling (better / as well as) today.

c) Andrew's work is (neater / the neatest) of all the people's in the office.

a) 同等比較の構文：as + 原級 + as ~で「～と同じぐらい」という意味になります。

b) 比較級の構文：比較級 + than が基本的な形となりますが，than が省略される場合もあります。その場合も比べる対象はどこかに明示されるので注意します。明示されてない場合は「現在よりも」「実際よりも」などの言葉を補って意味がとおれば比較級を選択します。b) は「今までより」という than ever が省略されています。

c) 最上級の構文：the + 最上級が基本的な形です。後ろに「～の中で」を意味する of + 複数名詞，in + 単数名詞のような比べる範囲を限定するような句がある場合は，その前はほとんどが the + 最上級です。

● その他の比較がらみの表現

例題 2（　）の中から正しい形を選びなさい。

a) Our prices are not (so high as / higher as) their prices.

b) The view from this hotel is (better than / better) that from that hotel.

c) The previous plan is (much better than / very better than) this plan.

d) He is three years (older / senior) to me.

e) This copier is (the easier / easier) to use of the two.

f) The older we grow, (the weaker / weaker) our eyesight becomes.

a) as + 原級 + as ~は多くの場合，否定文では so + 原級 + as ~となり「～ほど ... でない」という意味になります。

b) from that hotel の前の that は the view をさします。

c) 比較級の程度を強めるには much，far などを使います。

d) -or で終るラテン系の比較級は than ではなく to を使います。
他に，superior ⇔ inferior，junior ⇔ senior，prior などがあります。

e) のように比較されるものが of the two で 2 つに限定されている場合には比較級に the をつけます。

f) は the + 比較級 + SV，the + 比較級 + SV で「～すればするほど ... する」という構文です。

[Quiz]（　）の中から正しい形を選びなさい。

(1) (The eldest / The elder) of the two vice-presidents visited our office yesterday.

(2) It happened (prior to / prior than) his arrival.

(3) (As soon as / The sooner) you obtain the new software, the faster the new project will move forward.

PART 5: Select the best answer to complete each sentence.

1. To meet our sales quota this year, we should develop a ------- marketing plan than last year's.

(A) more practical
(B) practical
(C) more practically
(D) most practical

2. The quicker the delivery method you choose, ------- the fee you are billed.

(A) the high
(B) the higher
(C) high
(D) higher

3. The new fax machine doesn't work ------- the old one.

(A) as quickly
(B) quickly than
(C) so quickly as
(D) more quick than

4. The messenger will arrive at our office no ------- than 2:00 P.M.

(A) late
(B) latter
(C) latest
(D) later

5. For correcting typographical errors, it's ------- to use a computer than to use a dictionary.

(A) the most convenient
(B) the more convenient
(C) most convenient
(D) more convenient

1. Ⓐ Ⓑ Ⓒ Ⓓ **2.** Ⓐ Ⓑ Ⓒ Ⓓ **3.** Ⓐ Ⓑ Ⓒ Ⓓ **4.** Ⓐ Ⓑ Ⓒ Ⓓ **5.** Ⓐ Ⓑ Ⓒ Ⓓ

6. Robert commutes ------- of anyone in this workplace.

(A) the farther
(B) the far
(C) the farthest
(D) farther

7. As for retrieving new information, this computer is ------- of the two.

(A) efficient
(B) the more efficient
(C) the most efficient
(D) most efficient

8. His father is about three times ------- than he.

(A) oldest
(B) the oldest
(C) older
(D) as old as

9. Your document is ------- to Jim's regarding the solution to the problem.

(A) better
(B) the best
(C) superior
(D) the superior

10. Diamond House is ------- concert hall in this part of the country.

(A) the second largest
(B) second the largest
(C) the largest second
(D) second largest

6. Ⓐ Ⓑ Ⓒ Ⓓ **7.** Ⓐ Ⓑ Ⓒ Ⓓ **8.** Ⓐ Ⓑ Ⓒ Ⓓ **9.** Ⓐ Ⓑ Ⓒ Ⓓ **10.** Ⓐ Ⓑ Ⓒ Ⓓ

Unit 8

PART 4 録音メッセージ・広告

PART 6 比較がらみの表現②

PART 7 雑誌・新聞の記事

Listing Section　PART 4 録音メッセージ・広告

Technical Point

● 聞き手の立場になってメッセージを聞く

例題 録音メッセージを聞き，それに関する質問に対して最も適切なものを選びなさい。 33

What does Tom need to do first?

(A) Write a résumé

(B) Meet Pat Miller

(C) Go to the office

(D) Call Pat Miller

Ⓐ Ⓑ Ⓒ Ⓓ

留守番電話に残されたメッセージに関しては，メッセージが誰に宛てられたものか，何のために残されたメッセージなのか，などを正確に聞きとりましょう。もう一度聞いて，下線部に語句を書き入れなさい。

Hi, this is Pat Miller from TAT Advertisement. I'm calling for Tom Harris. We've received your 1.________________ form for this summer's internship program.
Your 2.________________ looks very impressive, and we would like to meet and talk with you in person. Would it be possible for you to come to our office for an 3.________________ sometime next week?
Please 4.__________ us at 555-0441, and we will talk about the details.

設問を先に読んで，聞かれていることをあらかじめ念頭において本文を聞きましょう。Tomが「最初に」することは何か，と言えば太字の箇所，つまり「電話をしてインタビューの詳細を決める」ことなので，正解は (D) になります。他の選択肢も本文中で取り扱われていますが，(A) は既に Tom が行ったこと，(B)，(C) は，電話でアポイントメントをとった後に行うことです。設問の first という語を見逃さないようにしましょう。

Training for the TOEIC L&R Test

PART 4: You will hear two short talks. Select the best answer to each question.

34

1. Who is the speaker?
(A) A flight attendant
(B) A travel agent
(C) An airline staff member
(D) A hotel clerk
Ⓐ Ⓑ Ⓒ Ⓓ

2. Why can't Ms. Madison stay at the hotel she wants to?
(A) It is overbooked.
(B) The room charge is beyond her budget.
(C) It is currently closed for renovation.
(D) They have only a few rooms available at the moment.
Ⓐ Ⓑ Ⓒ Ⓓ

3. What time will the office close tomorrow?
(A) At 5 P.M.
(B) At 6 P.M.
(C) At 7 P.M.
(D) It will be closed all day.
Ⓐ Ⓑ Ⓒ Ⓓ

35

4. What is being advertised?
(A) Laboratory equipment
(B) An academic institution
(C) A new website
(D) Information Technology programs
Ⓐ Ⓑ Ⓒ Ⓓ

5. What is NOT mentioned as a laboratory research subject?
(A) Astronomy
(B) The life sciences
(C) Physics
(D) Inquiry
Ⓐ Ⓑ Ⓒ Ⓓ

6. If you are a single parent, what can you get?
(A) A 10% discount
(B) A 20% discount
(C) A 30% discount
(D) A 60% discount
Ⓐ Ⓑ Ⓒ Ⓓ

Partial Dictation

Questions 1-3

Hello, Ms. Madison. This is Kathy Parks from Sun 1.________________. I am calling to give you an update on your trip to Tahiti. First of all, I'm 2.________________ that we weren't able to reserve the hotel you requested. The hotel is going through a large-scale renovation, and they are accepting a 3.________________________ of guests right now. I have a list of alternative accommodations for you to choose from, though. Please stop by at our office and take a look at it. About the flight, you've got what you have asked for. Please bring your passport with you when you visit us so that we can finalize the reservation. We are open from 10 A.M. to 8 P.M., Monday to Saturday, but we will close 4.____ tomorrow since it's a national holiday. Please give me a call before you come. Thank you.

Questions 4-6

Anderson 1.________________ is an extraordinary center of creativity, inquiry, and discovery. We offer over 250 courses, from anthropology through 2.________________, which are taught by leading experts in their fields. Our first-rate research laboratories put students at the forefront of discovery in the life sciences, physics, and 3.________________. All college experiences can be found here in Anderson College. We are currently offering special early registration rates for summer courses to those who apply before July 10th. There is also a 20% discount for seniors over sixty and a 30% discount for 4.___________________________. For more information, visit our website at www.anderson.edu.

Reading Section　PART 6 比較がらみの表現 ②

Technical Point

● さまざまな比較がらみの表現に慣れよう

例題（　　）の中から正しい形を選びなさい。

a) He likes her (all the better / the better all) for her frankness.

b) He had no (later / sooner) gone to bed than he heard someone knocking on the door.

c) (Most / Most of) items in the shop are on sale today.

d) This week, I will go to Tokyo and Osaka; the former to attend the leadership conference and (the latter / the later) to participate in the exhibition of our new products.

e) Jim can speak (as many as / as much as) six languages.

f) You cannot finish the job by tomorrow (other than / but than) by working overtime.

g) (As farther as / As far as) I know, he is the best-qualified person for the new position.

a) all the 比較級 for ~で「~のためにそれだけいっそう」という意味になります。

b) no sooner ~ than ... で「~するとすぐに…」という意味になります。No sooner のような否定語が文頭に出る時はその後の語順は疑問文と全く同じです (Unit 2 参照)。
(例：No sooner had he gone to bed than ....)。

c) most ~は「たいていの~」「大部分の~ 」という意味になります。Most of the ~も同じ意味になります。

d) 後者という意味を選びます。

e) 両方「~も」という意味ですが，language が可算名詞ということを考えます。

f)「~以外に」という意味です (but 単独であればそれも可)。

g) 後ろに SV を伴って「~する限り」という意味になります。原則として as (so) long as は時間や条件を，as (so) far as は程度・限界を表します。

[Quiz]（　　）の中から正しい形を選びなさい。

(1) (No sooner she had / No sooner had she) thanked the employees for their contributions to the new project than they broke out into loud applause.

(2) The situation became (all the worse for / the worse all for) the sudden change in the weather.

(3) Insofar (as / while) we are responsible for any negligence, we will refund your payment.

PART 6: Select the best answers to complete the text.
Questions 1-4 refer to the following article.

Last year, ------- 1. 20 million people in the USA planned at least one of their trips only a day or two ahead. ------- 2. Those travelers often find that unfilled seats and rooms are discounted at the last minute. In the United States today, ------- 3. the departure date draws, the less travel typically costs. Airlines, hotels, and cruise lines are eager to receive a few dollars for seats, rooms, or cabins that would otherwise go unfilled. As a result, they charge price-sensitive travelers ------- 4. if they book at the last minute.

1. (A) as many
(B) as many as
(C) as much
(D) as much as

2. (A) Then, they booked a flight and a hotel room at the last minute.
(B) Then, they canceled their reservation for the package tour.
(C) Then, they upgraded their tickets from economy class to business class.
(D) Then, they found it difficult to cancel a flight and a hotel room.

3. (A) near
(B) nearer
(C) the near
(D) the nearer

4. (A) less
(B) more
(C) worse
(D) better

1. Ⓐ Ⓑ Ⓒ Ⓓ **2.** Ⓐ Ⓑ Ⓒ Ⓓ **3.** Ⓐ Ⓑ Ⓒ Ⓓ **4.** Ⓐ Ⓑ Ⓒ Ⓓ

Reading Section PART 7 雑誌・新聞の記事

Technical Point ● まずタイトル，質問文，選択肢をざっと見てキーワードを探そう

タイトル，質問文，選択肢を見るとどのような分野の記事がかかれているのかが分かります。主題を問う問題を除くと，設問は文の流れに沿って作られている事が多いので，質問文を見ながら文章を検索して解いていきます。主題を問う問題は全部読んでから解いたほうがいいでしょう。また，設問は本文の言葉を言い換えて作っていることが多く，例えば，質問文が“What caused the change?” なら，本文中では “because of ~，thanks to ~，owing to ~，due to ~ ” などとなっていることがあります。英文読解力に加え，一般常識などの知識を基に推測しながら読み解いていくのがよいでしょう。

次のような，よく使われる質問文の例を線で結んでみましょう。

1) 肯定的に事実を問う質問 ・		・ a) The word “probably” in line 1 is closest in meaning to ...
2) 否定的に事実を問う質問 ・		・ b) What is this article mainly about?
3) 推測させる質問 ・		・ c) What can be inferred about people who have heartburn?
4) 同義語を問う質問 ・		・ d) What is NOT mentioned in the article?

Training for the TOEIC L&R Test

PART 7: Select the best answer to each question.
Questions 1-2 refer to the following notice.

Is It a Heart Attack or Heartburn?

Heartburn can—and probably does—happen to just about everyone from time to time. It is estimated that more than 60 million American adults experience heartburn once a month. About 25 million Americans suffer heartburn daily. Heartburn usually occurs after meals or when lying down and can last as long as several hours. It has been described as a burning feeling in the stomach area that moves up into the chest or throat, but that’s not always the case. “Every patient has his or her own perception of the symptoms,” explains Shawn Shaker, MD.

Since the sensation of heartburn is not the same for every person, it can sometimes be confused with heart pain.

But more commonly, heart pain is mistaken for heartburn. Only with a full medical evaluation it is possible to know definitely whether the pain you’re feeling is from heartburn or a heart attack, since the symptoms can be similar. If you experience heartburn two or more times a week for four weeks or more, then it’s a good idea to have a checkup.

1. What is NOT mentioned in this article?
(A) The number of Americans suffering from heartburn
(B) The number of Americans suffering from heart attacks
(C) The symptoms of heartburn
(D) The symptoms of a heart attack

2. How can you find out if you are suffering from heart pain or heartburn?
(A) By lying down after meals
(B) By having a burning feeling in the stomach area
(C) By having a full medical check-up
(D) By understanding your own perception of the symptoms

1. Ⓐ Ⓑ Ⓒ Ⓓ　　**2.** Ⓐ Ⓑ Ⓒ Ⓓ

Unit 9

PART 1 建物・乗り物と周りとの関係

PART 5 文と文との結びつきの表現①

Listening Section　PART 1　建物・乗り物と周りとの関係

Technical Point

● 建物中心の写真は周囲のものとの位置関係に注目

例題 1 次の写真を最も適切に描写している英文を選びなさい。 36

Ⓐ Ⓑ Ⓒ Ⓓ

下線部に聞きとった語句を書きなさい。

(A) Some artists are painting ________________ of the building.

(B) Some people are walking ___________________________ the building.

(C) The building is ________________.

(D) There are some trees growing ________________ the building.

建物中心の写真では特に前置詞を正確に聞きとり，周りにあるものとの位置関係を正しく描写しているものを選びます。ただし，(C) のような熟語表現には注意が必要です。

● 乗り物の写真では人物との関係に注目

例題 2 次の写真を最も適切に描写している英文を選びなさい。 37

Ⓐ Ⓑ Ⓒ Ⓓ

下線部に聞きとった語句を書きなさい。

(A) A man is opening the car's ______________.

(B) There is ____________________________ in the parking lot.

(C) Some people are ____________________________ the car.

(D) The car is parked on the ______________.

乗り物は人物が関わる場合が多いため，乗り物中心の写真は，まず人物も写っているかどうかを確認します。写っている場合は乗り物との関わり，つまり人物が乗り物に対してどこにいて何をしているかがよく出題されます。例題 2 の写真には車の後ろの方でいすに座っている人や立っている人が写っています。人と車の位置関係，人々の動作の両方が正しいものを選びます。人物が写っていない場合は例題 1 と同様に乗り物と周囲との位置関係が主に問われますが，その乗り物の特徴を描写することもあります。

Training for the TOEIC L&R Test

PART 1: Select the sentence that best describes what you see in each picture.

1. 38

Ⓐ Ⓑ Ⓒ Ⓓ

2. 39

Ⓐ Ⓑ Ⓒ Ⓓ

3. 40

Ⓐ Ⓑ Ⓒ Ⓓ

Partial Dictation

1. (A) The plane is stopped at the ______________________________.

(B) The plane is about to ______________________________.

(C) Some passengers are ______________________________ the plane.

(D) The plane is ______________________________ from the gate.

2. (A) All the pedestrians are ______________________________ at the flags.

(B) The steps lead up to the building with the ______________________________.

(C) There are ______________________________ waving on the top of the building.

(D) The palm tree is in ______________________________ the street.

3. (A) The convertible's ______________________________ is down.

(B) The man is ______________________________ the car.

(C) The cars are parked ______________________________.

(D) There is ______________________________ in the convertible.

Reading Section　PART 5　文と文との結びつきの表現 ①

Technical Point

● 文と文をつなぐには接続詞を使う

例題 1（　　）の中から正しい形を選びなさい。

a) Mr. Takahashi arrived (at / how / them / and) we started the meeting.

b) Larry didn't study very hard, (and / or / but) he had good exam results anyway.

c) I used to play baseball in this park (and / after / when / because) I was a child.

a) の（　　）の前後を見ると，どちらも主語 + 動詞を含む「文」です。つまり（　　）には文と文をつなぐ役割を持つ接続詞を入れなければなりません。例題の選択肢のうち接続詞は and だけです。「高橋氏が到着した」と「私たちは会議を始めた」を，そしてという意味の順接の and でつなぎます。

b) の選択肢はすべて接続詞ですが，前後の意味を確認すると「ラリーはあまり勉強しなかった」しかし「彼は試験でよい成績だった」とつながりますので，逆接の but にします。

c) は「私が子供だった」という後半の文が「この公園でよく野球をしたものだった」という前半の文に説明を加えています。例題ではwhenを選ぶと「私が子供だった時は」という意味の副詞節となり，最も自然につながります。このような接続詞の仲間には，「時」を表す before（～する前に），until（～するまで），「原因・理由」を表す because（～なので），「条件・譲歩」を表す if（もし～ならば），though（～であるけれども）などがあります。

● V-ing は時や理由などの意味を含んで文をつなぐ機能を持つ

例題 2（　　）の中から正しい形を選びなさい。

a) (To review / Reviewing / Review) the draft of my speech, I found some mistakes.

b) (Write / Writing / Written) in French, this paper is hard for me to understand.

c) While (stay / staying / stayed) in Yokohama, I met an old friend of mine.

a) では，「いくつかの間違いを見つけた」という後半の文から考えて，前半の英文とどのようにつながるか検討します。To review だと「(スピーチの原稿を) 見直すために」，また Review だと「見直しなさい」となり，いずれも後半の文にはつながりません。Reviewing を選ぶと「見直していると」という時を示す副詞句になり，後半の文に説明を加えています。このような V-ing（現在分詞）の句は文をつなぐ接続詞の働きがあり，また「時」，「理由」，「条件」，「付帯状況」，「譲歩」などの意味を含んでいます。

b) では，「フランス語で書かれているので」という意味を作るために受動態の分詞，つまり being written ~を用いますが，being は省略され，written で始めます。

c) は，文のつながりの意味をはっきりさせるため V-ing の前に接続詞をつけています。ここでは staying を選んで，「横浜に滞在している間」という意味にします。

Training for the TOEIC L&R Test

PART 5: Select the best answer to complete each sentence.

1. I'd like to attend the reception, ------- I have another appointment.

(A) and
(B) but
(C) when
(D) so

2. I'll approve his plan ------- others strongly oppose it.

(A) so
(B) however
(C) even though
(D) besides

3. ------- the sales manager was suddenly taken ill, I made his presentation for him.

(A) With
(B) Before
(C) Since
(D) But

4. ------- someone knocking on the door, we stopped talking.

(A) Hearing
(B) When to hear
(C) Heard
(D) Hear

5. ------- to most of her colleagues, Kate is a fast learner.

(A) Comparing
(B) Compare
(C) Compared
(D) Comparison

1. Ⓐ Ⓑ Ⓒ Ⓓ **2.** Ⓐ Ⓑ Ⓒ Ⓓ **3.** Ⓐ Ⓑ Ⓒ Ⓓ **4.** Ⓐ Ⓑ Ⓒ Ⓓ **5.** Ⓐ Ⓑ Ⓒ Ⓓ

6. We will purchase your product ------- you offer a three-year warranty.

(A) although
(B) even
(C) for
(D) provided

7. You should take experience into account ------- you consider people for a promotion.

(A) when
(B) because
(C) though
(D) but

8. ------- what was going on, we all sat silently waiting for instructions.

(A) Know
(B) Known
(C) Knowing not
(D) Not knowing

9. ------- an advertisement for a furnished studio apartment, she called the real estate agent.

(A) Found
(B) Been finding
(C) Having found
(D) Having been finding

10. More and more corporations are becoming involved in protecting the global environment ------- they realize that today, environmental practices greatly affect corporate image.

(A) however
(B) though
(C) when
(D) because

6. Ⓐ Ⓑ Ⓒ Ⓓ **7.** Ⓐ Ⓑ Ⓒ Ⓓ **8.** Ⓐ Ⓑ Ⓒ Ⓓ **9.** Ⓐ Ⓑ Ⓒ Ⓓ **10.** Ⓐ Ⓑ Ⓒ Ⓓ

Unit 10

PART 2 いろいろな形の問いかけに対応する

PART 6 文と文との結びつきの表現②

PART 7 求人広告と応募の手紙

Listening Section　PART 2　いろいろな形の問いかけに対応する

Technical Point

● 疑問文の形をとらない問いかけに対しては意味のつながりに特に注意する

例題 1 問いかけの文に対し応答として最も適切な英文を選びなさい。
下線部に聞きとった語句を書きなさい。　41

I heard the production manager will be back next week.

(A) ___________, he was.

(B) That's ______________________.

(C) So __________.

Ⓐ Ⓑ Ⓒ

例題 1 のように相手が疑問文ではなく平叙文で何かを言ったときも，その応答として自分の気持ちや意見を述べることがよくあります。ここでは「生産部長は来週帰ってくるそうです」という話題に対し，「それは良い知らせですね」という応答が最も自然です。このように事実や気持ちを述べた相手に対し，文の形よりも自然な意味のつながりで応答がどうなるかを予測しながら聞きましょう。

例題 2 問いかけの文に対し応答として最も適切な英文を選びなさい。
下線部に聞きとった語句を書きなさい。　42

Please send this document to Mr. Lee as soon as possible.

(A) It's coming __________.

(B) No, I ________________ it.

(C) Certainly. I'll do it _____________________.

Ⓐ Ⓑ Ⓒ

例題 2 は命令文の形をしていますが，依頼の意味です。「できるだけ早く書類を送って下さい」という問いかけに対し，「かしこまりました」と返答し，すぐに取りかかると述べている応答が正解です。問いかけに出てくる単語 send にひきずられると (B) と間違えます。このように問いかけにある語句と音の似ている語句が選択肢に入っていると，選んでしまうことがあります。文の形や個々の単語よりも問いかけの意味を正確にとらえ，最も自然につなぐ応答を選びます。

Training for the TOEIC L&R Test

PART 2: You will hear four questions and three possible responses to each. Select the best response to each question.

1. (A) (B) (C) **2.** (A) (B) (C) 43-46

3. (A) (B) (C) **4.** (A) (B) (C)

Partial Dictation

1. This room feels really __________ this morning.

(A) Yes, it's nearly __________.

(B) Yes, he is a member of our __________.

(C) You can __________ a window if you like.

2. You should probably take a __________ to the station.

(A) I think you are __________.

(B) I'm __________ that's the wrong direction.

(C) It's a 20-minute __________.

3. I was worried that he might ____________________ the presentation.

(A) Yes, he's always ______________.

(B) ______________ I.

(C) It started ______________.

4. I'd like you to ______________ the data entry errors before the afternoon meeting.

(A) I'll ______________ the data myself.

(B) Consider it ______________.

(C) Sorry, it's my ______________.

Reading Section　PART 6 文と文との結びつきの表現 ②

Technical Point

● さまざまな接続詞や V-ing を使って文と文を結ぶ

接続詞による連結：意味を確認しましょう。

a) when	b) while	c) before	d) after	e) until
f) since	g) because	h) if	i) unless	j) though

V-ing による連結：

動詞を現在分詞にして，接続詞の働きをさせる方法です。次の文の現在分詞にはどのような接続詞の意味が含まれるでしょうか。

1. Taking a bath, I hit upon an idea.
2. Turning to the right, you can see the bank.
3. Being an economist, he is interested in this paper.

受動態の Being を省略したり，また前に接続詞をおいて意味をはっきりさせたりする場合があります。次の文の意味を考えましょう。

4. Broken to pieces, the statue could not be displayed.
5. While reading, he doesn't want to be disturbed.

[Quiz]（　　）の中から正しい形を選びなさい。

(1) You should get a ticket (and / but / before / unless) you enter the stadium.

(2) (To see / See / Seeing / Seen) the mailman, the dog began barking.

(3) When (leave / leaving / left) this room, turn off the light.

● 文選択問題は，全体の流れをつかんでからその段落に共通する内容の文を選ぶ。

> 英文は段落の最初に話題を提供する「トピックセンテンス」があり，同じ段落中は同じ話題が続きます。そのため，段落の最初や途中の空所に文を入れる「文選択問題」を解く場合，選択肢からその段落に共通する内容の文を探すのが手掛かりの１つとなります。また，他の段落のトピックを選択肢から外す消去法も有効です。
>
> 文選択問題は，4 問中の何番目にあってもそこで止まって解くのではなく，全体を読み，他の段落のトピックも知ってから解くと誤答が少なくなります。

Training for the TOEIC L&R Test

PART 6: Select the best answers to complete the text.
Questions 1-4 refer to the following guide.

INSTRUCTION PERMITS

You must have an instruction permit while you are learning to drive a motor vehicle on public roads. When ------- (**1.**) for a permit, you must pass the written test. ------- (**2.**) The Department of Licenses may issue a second renewal ------- (**3.**) you show steady progress in improving your driving ability. The permit is only valid ------- (**4.**) you are driving within this state and there is a licensed driver with at least five years' driving experience seated beside you.

1. (A) apply
(B) to apply
(C) applying
(D) applied
Ⓐ Ⓑ Ⓒ Ⓓ

2. (A) The driving test will be given in a vehicle you provide.
(B) You must be at least 16 years old to apply for a permit.
(C) You should arrive 15 minutes early for your drive test.
(D) The permit is valid for one year and one renewal is allowed.
Ⓐ Ⓑ Ⓒ Ⓓ

3. (A) and
(B) if
(C) unless
(D) how
Ⓐ Ⓑ Ⓒ Ⓓ

4. (A) when
(B) on
(C) because
(D) but
Ⓐ Ⓑ Ⓒ Ⓓ

Reading Section　PART 7 求人広告と応募の手紙

Technical Point ● 求人広告と応募の手紙では，職務と採用条件に注目し，応募者の資質と比べる

「求人 (Help Wanted)」は広告文の一種で，新聞には案内広告 (classified ad) のページに簡潔な英文で掲載されています。TOEIC でも似たようなスタイルでよく出題されます。まず職種と職務内容 (duties または responsibilities)，学歴や経験，資格や技能などの採用条件（requirements)，さらに応募方法を読みとります。

「応募の手紙」とは，履歴書 (résumé) と一緒に送る添え状 (cover letter) のことで，応募者として自分を印象づける大切な役割があります。そのため，採用してもらうために応募者の能力や業績を会社側の条件に結びつける内容になっています。

このような特徴を持つ２つの文書が出題されたら，特に会社側の条件 (requirements) と応募者の資質 (qualifications) が合うかどうかを比べて読む必要があります。

Training for the TOEIC L&R Test

PART 7: Select the best answer to each question.
Questions 1-5 refer to the following advertisement and e-mail.

HELP WANTED: A MAJOR U.S. PHARMACEUTICAL COMPANY is seeking an experienced receptionist. The ideal candidate will have strong motivation, more than 2 years' experience, good command of Japanese and English, with PC skills. Please send résumé with cover letter by e-mail to Ellen Clark, admini@sli.com or by fax at 035-555-1010.

SLI Corporation, Tokyo.

To:	Ellen Clark <admini@sli.com>
Subject:	Job Application
Attachment:	Résumé

Dear Ms. Clark:

I am writing in response to your recent newspaper ad. I would like to offer myself as a candidate for the position of receptionist at SLI Corporation, Tokyo.

I have been working at Kobe Trading, Tokyo Branch, as a receptionist for the last two years. In my current position, I have greatly improved my English conversation skills as I have had dealings with many customers from all over the world, particularly England and the United States. I have also been using a computer to collect feedback from customers, so my PC skills are excellent. I believe I can make the most of my abilities and experience in a foreign-affiliated company such as yours.

I have enclosed my résumé as an attachment to this e-mail.
I look forward to hearing from you at your earliest convenience.

Sincerely,
Yoko Nishino

1. What is NOT a requirement for the position?

(A) Fluency in Japanese and English
(B) A good knowledge of pharmaceuticals
(C) Working experience as a receptionist for more than 2 years
(D) Ability to work with computers

2. How should people apply for the position?

(A) Send a résumé to SLI Corporation by regular mail
(B) Send a résumé and cover letter to SLI Corporation by e-mail or fax
(C) Visit SLI Corporation and meet Ellen Clark in person
(D) By telephone

3. Where does Yoko probably live?

(A) Tokyo
(B) England
(C) Kobe
(D) The United States

4. How has Yoko improved her English?

(A) By studying abroad
(B) By talking with customers in English
(C) By taking special courses in her current company
(D) By traveling abroad, particularly to the U.S.

5. Which of the following is NOT true?

(A) Yoko meets all the necessary requirements.
(B) Yoko has sent her résumé by e-mail.
(C) SLI Corporation is affiliated with a foreign company.
(D) Yoko is no longer working at Kobe Trading Co.

1. Ⓐ Ⓑ Ⓒ Ⓓ **2.** Ⓐ Ⓑ Ⓒ Ⓓ **3.** Ⓐ Ⓑ Ⓒ Ⓓ **4.** Ⓐ Ⓑ Ⓒ Ⓓ **5.** Ⓐ Ⓑ Ⓒ Ⓓ

Unit 11

PART 3 同僚との多様なやりとり

PART 5 V-ing と V-ed の使い分け ①

Listening Section　PART 3 同僚との多様なやりとり

Technical Point ● オフィス用語に慣れて同僚との多様な話題を聞きとる

例題 会話を聞き，それに関する質問に対して最も適切なものを選びなさい。 47

Where does this conversation most likely take place?
(A) At Sarah's house
(B) On the telephone
(C) At the office in Tokyo
(D) At a restaurant in Tokyo

Ⓐ Ⓑ Ⓒ Ⓓ

「どこで会話がかわされていると思われるか」が問われています。週末の予定を尋ねることから始まる日常会話のようですが，空所を埋めながら最後まで注意して聞いてみましょう。

M: What are you going to do this weekend, Sarah?
W: I'm 1._________________ Kuala Lumpur on Friday afternoon. I'll be back in Tokyo on Tuesday.
M: Kuala Lumpur? I've been there twice. You'll really enjoy the food and the beach.
W: Sounds nice, but it's not for a vacation. I have to visit the 2._________________ there and meet the staff. Anyway, let's 3._________________ this document. I don't want to have to work overtime again.

会話問題ではオフィス内の会話が多く出題されますが，例題のように日常の場面のような問いかけから始まり，話題の中心が本来の仕事の内容でない場合は，最後まで場所がわかりにくくなっています。例題では，網掛け部分の be back in Tokyo, document, work overtime などの語句がヒントとなり，この会話は「東京のオフィスで」かわされていることがわかります。
職場の同僚との間では，仕事の進み具合を尋ねる，物の貸し借りをする，道具の使い方を尋ねる，休暇を代わってもらう，ランチに誘う，など仕事に直接は関わらないものの，オフィス内ならではの会話もあります。話題はさまざまですが，例題のようにオフィス特有の語句がキーワードになることがあるので，日常用語に加えて慣れておきましょう。

● 発言意図問題では必ず先読みをして前後の情報に集中する

PART 3 では話し手の発言の意図，動機などを問う問題が出題されることがあります。設問形式は What does the man mean / imply when he says, "XXX"? や Why does the man say, "XXX"? など特徴があります。この "XXX" の部分を先読みして，待ち伏せする気持ちで集中して聞きましょう。発言の意図をくみ取るヒントはその発言の前後にあることが多いからです。

Training for the TOEIC L&R Test

PART 3: You will hear two short conversations. Select the best answer to each question.

48

1. What does the man mean when he says, "No problem"?
(A) He is not in trouble right now.
(B) He would like to give his seat to her.
(C) He is happy to cancel this afternoon's meeting.
(D) He is willing to attend the meeting this afternoon.
Ⓐ Ⓑ Ⓒ Ⓓ

2. Who caught a cold?
(A) The woman
(B) The man
(C) The woman's little girl
(D) The babysitter
Ⓐ Ⓑ Ⓒ Ⓓ

3. Which of these is NOT mentioned as a cold symptom?
(A) Sore throat
(B) Runny nose
(C) Cough
(D) Fever
Ⓐ Ⓑ Ⓒ Ⓓ

49

4. What does the woman imply when she says, "Good for him"?
(A) She's going to miss Tim.
(B) She wishes Tim's health.
(C) She's been wanting to replace Tim.
(D) She is happy to hear about Tim's promotion.
Ⓐ Ⓑ Ⓒ Ⓓ

5. Where do they probably work?
(A) Both of them work in the sales department.
(B) Both of them work in the human resources department.
(C) The man works in sales, and the woman works in human resources.
(D) The man works in human resources, and the woman works in sales.
Ⓐ Ⓑ Ⓒ Ⓓ

6. Which of the following is probably true about Tim?
(A) He is interested in staying in the human resources department.
(B) He is already working in the sales department.
(C) He thinks sales will be more challenging.
(D) He lacks ability.
Ⓐ Ⓑ Ⓒ Ⓓ

Partial Dictation

Questions 1-3

W: Say, Ed, I'm not going to be able to 1.________________ to this afternoon's meeting. Could you sit in for me?

M: No problem, Becky, but may I ask why?

W: Well, my daughter 2.____________________ a cold last night. I gave her some medicine we had at home, but it doesn't seem 3.______________________. My babysitter 4.________________ and says my daughter has a fever and sore throat, and her cough's getting worse.

M: You'd better run home then and take her to 5.______________________. Don't worry about the meeting.

Questions 4-6

M: Did you hear about Tim? He got a promotion. Starting next month, he'll be head of the 1.__________________________.

W: Good for him. 2.___________________ he looks so happy these days.

M: He's been wanting to 3._________________ a more challenging job. I think he will be able to 4.________________________________ in sales a lot more than he can here in human resources.

W: Have you heard if the company has 5.________________________ to replace him here?

Reading Section　PART 5 V-ing と V-ed の使い分け ①

Technical Point

● 「する」のか「される」のか

例題 1（　　）の中から正しい形を選びなさい。

a) Who is the secretary (working / worked) with Mr. Lee?

b) What is the language (speaking / spoken) in Australia?

動詞の形，現在分詞 (V-ing) か過去分詞 (V-ed) を選ぶためには，「する」「される」という能動か受動かの判断がポイントとなり，「誰（何）が」という動作の主体が，「する」のか，「される」のか意味を確認して区別します。動詞の形は，「する」の意味なら現在分詞（V-ing），「される」の意味なら過去分詞（V-ed）を選びます。

[Quiz]（　　）の中から正しい形を選びなさい。

(1) She usually eats (frying / fried) eggs for breakfast.

(2) Do you know the man (standing / stood) at the front desk?

● 感情や状態を表現するには

例題 2（　　）の中から正しい形を選びなさい。

a) I was (surprising / surprised) when I heard the company was closing down.

b) The details of the accident were (shocking / shocked).

surprise，shock はそれぞれ「驚かせる」，「衝撃を与える」という意味で，感情や状態を引き起こす他動詞です。これを V-ing と V-ed に変化させると，surprising「驚かせるような」，surprised「驚かされた」shocking「衝撃的な」，shocked「衝撃を与えられた」という意味になります。a) の「私」は「驚かされた」という意味，また b) の「事故の詳細」は「衝撃的な」ものだったという意味を選びます。

[Quiz]（　　）の中から正しい形を選びなさい。

(1) What you've just said is very (confusing / confused) for us.

(2) We were (thrilling / thrilled) to hear about your success.

PART 5: Select the best answer to complete each sentence.

1. Was your daughter ------- about her birthday party?

(A) exciting
(B) excitedly
(C) excitement
(D) excited

2. The machine's noise was so ------- that we could hardly work.

(A) annoyed
(B) much annoyed
(C) annoyance
(D) annoying

3. The 15-year-old boy reportedly ------- the gunpowder and explosive device himself.

(A) make
(B) making
(C) made
(D) to make

4. It's not ------- that this company was able to produce such a fine natural skin care product.

(A) surprising
(B) surprise
(C) surprised
(D) to surprise

5. The library is filled with people ------- all kinds of things.

(A) who reads
(B) and read
(C) to read
(D) reading

1. Ⓐ Ⓑ Ⓒ Ⓓ **2.** Ⓐ Ⓑ Ⓒ Ⓓ **3.** Ⓐ Ⓑ Ⓒ Ⓓ **4.** Ⓐ Ⓑ Ⓒ Ⓓ **5.** Ⓐ Ⓑ Ⓒ Ⓓ

6. Since last year, consumers have been able to buy green tea in plastic bottles ------- from Shanghai by Japanese companies.

(A) shipping
(B) that ship
(C) shipped
(D) shipment

7. Taking the family abroad can be an ------- experience for everyone.

(A) enriched
(B) enrichment
(C) enriching
(D) enrichment by

8. Ten students were hospitalized for injuries, including two boys with ------ legs.

(A) breaking
(B) broke
(C) broken
(D) broked

9. Fortunately, the training program ------- at the meeting was accepted immediately.

(A) propose
(B) proposing
(C) proposal
(D) proposed

10. Many of the 1,500 ------- companies that we surveyed were using outside providers.

(A) list up
(B) listing
(C) list
(D) listed

6. Ⓐ Ⓑ Ⓒ Ⓓ **7.** Ⓐ Ⓑ Ⓒ Ⓓ **8.** Ⓐ Ⓑ Ⓒ Ⓓ **9.** Ⓐ Ⓑ Ⓒ Ⓓ **10.** Ⓐ Ⓑ Ⓒ Ⓓ

Unit 12

PART 4 案内放送

PART 6 V-ing と V-ed の使い分け ②

PART 7 お知らせ文

Listing Section　PART 4　案内放送

Technical Point

● 空港・機内での案内放送は，時刻，目的地，変更点に注意

案内放送とは，空港や機内，駅や電車内，バスターミナルなどの交通機関に関わる場所やデパート，学校，図書館，映画館，遊園地など，人が集まるさまざまな場所で流れる放送のことです。まずどんな場所かを判断することが大切です。

例題 案内放送を聞き，それに関する質問に対して最も適切なものを選びなさい。　50

Which of the following has been changed for flight 884?

(A) Departure time and destination

(B) Departure gate and destination

(C) Departure time and departure gate

(D) Departure time and arrival gate

Ⓐ Ⓑ Ⓒ Ⓓ

空港，機内での案内放送はよく出題されます。フライトの出発や到着時刻，目的地，搭乗時刻，ゲートなどの情報のほか，変更点とその原因，さらにそれに応じた乗客への指示を含むことがあります。例題をもう一度聞き，下線部に語句を書き入れながら「何が変更されたか」を考えてみましょう。

May I have your attention, please?　Flight 884 to Chicago will 1. ________________ at 4:30 P.M. instead of 3:20 P.M. due to heavy winds. We'd also like to 2. ________________ passengers on this flight that the departure gate has been 3. ________________ from Gate 23 to Gate 33. Flight 884 to Chicago will be ready for boarding at Gate 33 in thirty minutes. We apologize for any 4. ________________ that this may cause our passengers.

フライトの出発にあたり，天候の理由から時刻の変更，それに伴うゲート番号を知らせる空港内の案内放送です。変更点は，下線 1 の depart から出発時刻の departure time と，網掛け部分 departure gate の 2 つであることがわかります。

Training for the TOEIC L&R Test

PART 4: You will hear two short talks. Select the best answer to each question.

51

1. Where does this announcement take place?
(A) At an airport
(B) At a shopping center
(C) At a school
(D) At a bookstore
Ⓐ Ⓑ Ⓒ Ⓓ

2. Which of the following is NOT true about the children?
(A) They are lost in the mall.
(B) The older boy is called Jack.
(C) The younger boy has blue eyes.
(D) Both boys are wearing T-shirts and pants.
Ⓐ Ⓑ Ⓒ Ⓓ

3. What should the parents of the lost children do?
(A) Go to the big bear.
(B) Go to the service counter.
(C) Go to the toy store.
(D) Go to the bookstore.
Ⓐ Ⓑ Ⓒ Ⓓ

52

4. Who is making this announcement?
(A) A pilot
(B) A flight attendant
(C) A tour guide
(D) A gate attendant
Ⓐ Ⓑ Ⓒ Ⓓ

5. How long will the flight take?
(A) 6 hours and 23 minutes
(B) 7 hours and 15 minutes
(C) 7 hours and 50 minutes
(D) 8 hours and 25 minutes
Ⓐ Ⓑ Ⓒ Ⓓ

6. Which of the following is NOT true about this flight?
(A) There will be a little turbulence on the way.
(B) The flight attendants will serve drinks and a snack.
(C) It will arrive in Kuala Lumpur on time.
(D) The flight has been delayed due to bad weather.
Ⓐ Ⓑ Ⓒ Ⓓ

Partial Dictation

Questions 1-3

Attention, Northeast Mall shoppers. We have two 1.____________________. One is a four-year-old boy 2._______________ Jack. He is wearing a yellow T-shirt and white pants. The other child is a boy about three years old in a white cap, white T-shirt, and 3.__________________. He has brown eyes and brown, curly hair. Both boys were found near the big bear displayed 4.__________________ Jerry's Toy Store, but they do not appear to be together or related. If your child fits the description of either child, please come to the 5.____________________________
next to the bookstore located on the 6.__________________. Thank you very much.

Questions 4-6

Good afternoon, ladies and gentlemen. This is your 1.___________________. On behalf of the 2.______________ of flight 623, I'd like to welcome you aboard our nonstop service to Kuala Lumpur. Today's flight will take approximately seven hours and fifteen minutes. I've been informed that there will be some stormy weather 3.___________________ Kuala Lumpur, so we can expect a little 4.____________________. I have just turned off the seat-belt sign, so you are free to get up and move about the cabin. However, please keep your seatbelts fastened when in your seats. We should be arriving in Kuala Lumpur 5.______________________ at 8:25 P.M. local time. Our flight attendants will soon 6.______________________ with drinks and a snack, and we will now begin our in-flight movie service. Enjoy your flight, and thank you for flying with us.

Reading Section　PART 6 V-ing と V-ed の使い分け ②

Technical Point ● 目的語のあとも「する」「される」で区別する

例題（　　）の中から正しい形を選びなさい。

a) She had the computer (carrying / carried) to her room by a delivery person.

b) They heard someone (knocking / knocked) on the door.

c) We had our grandmother (examining / examined) at the clinic.

現在分詞 (V-ing) か過去分詞 (V-ed) かを選ぶためには,「誰（何）が」という動作の主体が「する」のか,「される」のかを判断しますが，例題ではこの判断の基準となる主体が目的語になっています。

a) は「彼女はそのコンピュータを配達人に部屋まで運んでもらった」という意味です。英文の中の carry の主体は「コンピュータ」で,「運ばれる」側となるので過去分詞を選びます。

b) は主体の「誰か」が「ノックしている」ので現在分詞を選びます。目的語が「物」ならそのあとは過去分詞,「人」ならそのあとは現在分詞，という判断は違うことがありますので注意します。

c) は「私たちはそのクリニックで祖母を診察してもらった」という意味です。目的語は「人」ですが,「診察される」側となるので過去分詞を選びます。

このように，目的語が主体の場合もそれが「人」か「物」か，だけで判断せず，あとに続く動作について「する」側なら現在分詞,「される」側なら過去分詞を選びます。

[Quiz]（　　）の中から正しい形を選びなさい。

Keep the front door (double-locking / double-locked) when you are in your room.

Training for the TOEIC L&R Test

PART 6: Select the best answers to complete the text.
Questions 1-4 refer to the following article.

July 18

Dear Ms. Takao,

I am sorry I have kept you ------- **1.** for this reply, but I have been on a business trip to Sendai for the past week.

I am happy to welcome you to the teaching staff of Condon College Japan, and I want to assist you in any way that I can. Starting this fall, you will be teaching ELS 217 Grammar, which is our Grammar II class. ------- **2.** This is a four-credit required class.

Please find ------- **3.** copies of the most recent course syllabus and the textbook ------- **4.** in the course. If you have any questions, please stop by my office or e-mail me at cathw@ccj.com.

Please have a good rest of the summer, and I'll see you in September.

Sincerely,
Cathleen Walters

1. (A) wait
(B) waited
(C) waiting
(D) to wait

2. (A) You need 124 credits in order to graduate.
(B) Three late arrivals are counted as one absence.
(C) This class meets on Monday and Wednesday mornings from 10:00 to 11:30 A.M.
(D) Please do not forget to bring photo ID when you come to the class.

3. (A) enclose
(B) enclosing
(C) to enclose
(D) enclosed

4. (A) use
(B) used
(C) using
(D) to use

---

1. Ⓐ Ⓑ Ⓒ Ⓓ　**2.** Ⓐ Ⓑ Ⓒ Ⓓ　**3.** Ⓐ Ⓑ Ⓒ Ⓓ　**4.** Ⓐ Ⓑ Ⓒ Ⓓ

Reading Section　PART 7 お知らせ文

Technical Point

● 「お知らせ」文は対象，目的，条件に注目

「お知らせ」とは，集合住宅や学校，公共施設などの掲示板に貼られたり手紙が配布されたりして人々が目にする案内文のことです。内容はイベント情報，規則の変更，施設内設備の説明などさまざまです。「誰」に対する情報か，「目的」は何か，をまず読みとります。

情報を読みとるための正しい質問文を選びましょう。

1) 対象 ・　　・ a) What do you need if you want to attend the party?
2) 内容 ・　　・ b) Why has this notice been written?
3) 条件 ・　　・ c) To whom is this notice directed?
4) 目的 ・　　・ d) What is this notice about?

● 「文の位置選択問題」

文書中に空所が 4 か所（[1], [2], [3], [4]）あり，提示された文を正しい位置に入れる問題があります。正解の場所を探す手がかりとして，提示文中に代名詞 (this, that など) があればそれが示す語句が空所前にあるかどうか，接続副詞 (therefore, however など) があれば空所前後の意味のつながりに注意します。文書全体の流れをつかみながら精読するとともに，提示文の中の語句などに注目しましょう。

Training for the TOEIC L&R Test

PART 7: Select the best answer to each question.
Questions 1-3 refer to the following notice.

Temporary Water Outage

On Monday November 1st, it will be necessary to temporarily shut off the water line for buildings A1 and A2 due to an emergency boiler and plumbing repair. – [1] – We recently installed a new cooling system. – [2] – The contractors who installed the system deemed the repair necessary after discovering a leak in the boiler room.

The repair is expected to begin at 9 a.m. and be completed by 3 p.m. As soon as the repair is completed, regular water services will be restored. Although we do not expect for the repair to affect buildings B1 and B2, we wanted to make everyone aware in case you experience any issues during this process. – [3] –

We apologize for this inconvenience and appreciate your understanding. – [4] – If you have any questions, please do not hesitate to contact the operator below:

Customer Service: 800-555-7000

1. To whom is this notice directed?
(A) Residents in buildings A1 and A2
(B) Residents in buildings A1, A2, B1, and B2
(C) Repairpersons for a boiler system
(D) An operator at customer service
Ⓐ Ⓑ Ⓒ Ⓓ

2. Why is the repair considered necessary?
(A) Due to the upgrading of city water meters
(B) Due to the installing of a new boiler system
(C) Because the water line was shut off.
(D) Because a problem was found in the boiler room
Ⓐ Ⓑ Ⓒ Ⓓ

3. In which of the positions marked [1], [2], [3], and [4] does the following sentence best belong? "This will temporarily interrupt the water supply to both buildings."
(A) [1]
(B) [2]
(C) [3]
(D) [4]
Ⓐ Ⓑ Ⓒ Ⓓ

Unit 13

PART 1 複数の人物の様子

PART 5 まぎらわしい動詞の語形・意味・語法

Listening Section　PART 1　複数の人物の様子

Technical Point

● 複数人物の描写を聞きとる

例題 1 次の写真を最も適切に描写している英文を選びなさい。 53

Ⓐ Ⓑ Ⓒ Ⓓ

下線部に聞きとった語句を書きなさい。

(A) They are ________________ on sofas.

(B) They are ________________ the table.

(C) They are ________________ hands.

(D) They are watching ________________________.

複数の人物が写っている場合，全員が同じ動作（格好）をしているのか，それともそのうちの何人かが異なった動作をしているのかを見極める必要があります。例題 1 は，全員が同じ動作をしています。

● 全員が同じ動作をしていない場合には，数を表す語に注意

例題 2 次の写真を最も適切に描写している英文を選びなさい。 54

Ⓐ Ⓑ Ⓒ Ⓓ

下線部に聞きとった語句を書きなさい。

(A) They are all standing around the ______________________.

(B) They are having a picnic on the ______________________.

(C) Two women are sitting on the ______________________.

(D) They are ______________________ side by side in the park.

写真に写っている複数の人物のうち，2人が座っています。したがって，(A) の all や (C) の two women などの数を表す語に注意する必要があります。

Training for the TOEIC L&R Test

PART 1: Select the sentence that best describes what you see in each picture.

1. 55

Ⓐ Ⓑ Ⓒ Ⓓ

2. 56

Ⓐ Ⓑ Ⓒ Ⓓ

3. 57

Ⓐ Ⓑ Ⓒ Ⓓ

Partial Dictation

1. (A) The people are ______________________________ to catch the bus.

(B) Some people are ______________________________ the street.

(C) Someone is ______________________________ the sidewalk.

(D) ______________________________ on this street is very heavy.

2. (A) They are waiting for a train on the ______________________________.

(B) Vendors are ______________________________ some merchandise.

(C) One person is carrying an ______________________________.

(D) Everyone is looking at the man by the ______________________________.

3. (A) They are ______________________________ on the beach.

(B) Most of the people are sitting on the ______________________________ in the park.

(C) The audience is giving the performer a big round of ________________________ ____________________.

(D) They are sitting in a big ______________________________.

Reading Section　PART 5　まぎらわしい動詞の語形・意味・語法

Technical Point

● 形がまぎらわしい動詞は活用もしっかり覚える

例題 1（　　）の中から正しい形を選びなさい。

a) As soon as Rick came home, he (lie / lay / laid / lain) on the sofa.

b) Sue gently (lie / lay / laid / lain) her baby on the bed.

例題のように，活用させると形がまぎらわしい動詞があります。a) は「(彼はソファに) 横になった」という意味の自動詞で，lie の過去形の lay，b) は「(赤ちゃんを) 寝かせた」という意味の他動詞で，lay の過去形の laid を選びます。動詞の活用も正確に覚えましょう。

lie-lay-lain「横になる」，lay-laid-laid「横たえる，置く」，
rise-rose-risen「上がる，昇る」，raise-raised-raised「～を上げる，～を育てる」，
arise-arose-arisen「起こる，高まる」，arouse-aroused-aroused「～を引き起こす」

● 意味がまぎらわしい動詞はあとに続く目的語と場面を考えて使い分ける

例題 2（　　）の中から正しい語を選びなさい。

a) How long can we (borrow / rent / use) videos from this library?

b) May I (borrow / rent / use) the bathroom?

例題のように，似たような意味で，まぎらわしい動詞があります。a) は「図書館から無料で借りる」ので borrow，b) は「お借りしてもいいですか」と訳しますが「その場で使わせてもらう」ので use を選びます。rent は「有料で一定期間借りる，貸す」場合に使います。あとに続く目的語と場面を考えて使い分けましょう。

write「文字を書く」，draw「線で描く」，paint「絵の具で描く」，forget「～を忘れる」，
leave「(具体的な場所に) 置き忘れる」

● 語法がまぎらわしい動詞は例文ごと覚える

例題 3（　　）の中から正しい語を選びなさい。

a) Our boss often (says / tells) “collaboration” in his morning speech.

b) He (said / told / talked / spoke) me that he was going to attend this meeting.

選択肢は「言う，話す」という意味の動詞ですが，使い方（語法）が決まっています。

a) のように，“collaboration” という話される言葉そのものを目的語にしている場合は say を使います。tell は話の内容を伝える場合に使います。

b) は「人に～と言う」という場合ですが，選択肢にある動詞の主な語法は，say + that ～，say to + 人 + that ～，tell + 人 + that ～，talk to + 人，speak to + 人となります。例文の（　　）の直後に me があることに注目し，動詞 + 人 + that ～の形にできる told を選びます。語法を確認して簡潔な例文を覚えたほうがいいでしょう。

PART 5: Select the best answer to complete each sentence.

1. If you have a question, please ------- your hand.

(A) rise
(B) rose
(C) raise
(D) arise

2. Come in and ------- your child on this examination table.

(A) lie
(B) laid
(C) lay
(D) lying

3. Don't ------- to me while I'm reading.

(A) say
(B) tell
(C) told
(D) speak

4. Mr. Nakagawa ------- the documents on his secretary's desk.

(A) leave
(B) remained
(C) left
(D) disappeared

5. Since I didn't know where the office was, I asked her to ------- a map.

(A) draw
(B) write
(C) paint
(D) dictate

1. Ⓐ Ⓑ Ⓒ Ⓓ **2.** Ⓐ Ⓑ Ⓒ Ⓓ **3.** Ⓐ Ⓑ Ⓒ Ⓓ **4.** Ⓐ Ⓑ Ⓒ Ⓓ **5.** Ⓐ Ⓑ Ⓒ Ⓓ

6. In some areas in Japan, the temperature ------- above 40°C last summer.

(A) rose
(B) raised
(C) arouse
(D) aroused

7. May I ------- this dictionary for a while? I'll return it as soon as I'm done with it.

(A) rent
(B) hire
(C) lend
(D) borrow

8. In the last election, Mr. Hudson, 62, ------- two other candidates for governor.

(A) beat
(B) overcame
(C) won
(D) pressed

9. Ms. Hamilton ------- that we should fill out this application form as soon as possible.

(A) told
(B) talked
(C) said
(D) spoke

10. Mr. Taylor is the first chief executive officer of this leading company, which was ------- by a few college students in 1985.

(A) found
(B) build
(C) finding
(D) founded

6. Ⓐ Ⓑ Ⓒ Ⓓ **7.** Ⓐ Ⓑ Ⓒ Ⓓ **8.** Ⓐ Ⓑ Ⓒ Ⓓ **9.** Ⓐ Ⓑ Ⓒ Ⓓ **10.** Ⓐ Ⓑ Ⓒ Ⓓ

Unit 14

PART 2 How と Why の広がる意味とその応答

PART 6 まぎらわしい前置詞の表現

PART 7 説明文とレシピ

Listening Section　PART 2　How と Why の広がる意味とその応答

Technical Point

● How の直後の語をよく聞いて正しい意味をつかみ，まぎらわしい応答につられないこと

例題 1 問いかけの文に対し応答として最も適切な英文を選びなさい。
下線部に聞きとった語句を書きなさい。　58

How many e-mails do you send every day?

(A) Between ______________________.

(B) ______________________, on average.

(C) I ______________________ last week.　Ⓐ　Ⓑ　Ⓒ

How は，単独で使って「どのように，～の方法」と状態や手段を尋ねる文を作るほか，形容詞や副詞を伴って how many「いくつの～」，how long「どれくらいの時間～」，how far「どれくらい遠く～」，how often「どれくらいの頻度で～」という意味を作ります。また，how come「なぜ～」，how about「～はどうですか」など意味を広げることがあります。How の直後の語を聞きのがさないようにしましょう。ただし，例題 1 では「数」が問われていることがわかったとしても，選択肢の全てに数字が含まれているのでまぎらわしい応答です。(B) はかかる時間，(C) は先週送ったメールの数を答えているので不正解です。

● Why に対しては because につられず理由としてつながる応答を選ぶ

例題 2 問いかけの文に対し応答として最も適切な英文を選びなさい。
下線部に聞きとった語句を書きなさい。　59

Why was the forum canceled?

(A) Because he has never been to one ______________.

(B) I hear most of the ______________ caught the flu.

(C) I ______________ the forum, too.　Ⓐ　Ⓑ　Ⓒ

例題 2 は「公開討論会が中止された」理由を尋ねています。(A) は「彼は公開討論会に行ったことがないから」という意味なので，Because で始まっていますが理由としてつながりません。また，(C) は中止されたはずの討論会に「参加しました」と言っているので，矛盾している応答です。(B) の「ほとんどのパネリストがインフルエンザにかかった」ことが討論会中止の理由になっているので，これが正解となります。このように，理由を尋ねる Why 疑問文に対しては，because の有無にかかわらず，正しい理由を選ぶように注意して聞きましょう。また，Why で始まる文でも Why don't you ～？は「理由」ではなく「勧誘」や「提案」を意味します。このような決まった表現にも注意が必要です。

Training for the TOEIC L&R Test

PART 2: You will hear four questions and three possible responses to each. Select the best response to each question.

1. Ⓐ Ⓑ Ⓒ 2. Ⓐ Ⓑ Ⓒ 60-63

3. Ⓐ Ⓑ Ⓒ 4. Ⓐ Ⓑ Ⓒ

Partial Dictation

1. __________ are you going to the airport tonight?

(A) Sheila will give me ________________.

(B) It takes ________________ to get there.

(C) My flight is at ________________.

2. Why did Mr. Walker ________________ to the Osaka office?

(A) He ________________ the office every day.

(B) Because the new Osaka office will open next ____________.

(C) Osaka's his ____________________.

3. ________________ will the meeting begin?

(A) Sorry, she won't be able to ________________.

(B) It'll ________________ at least two hours.

(C) It should get underway ________________ 30 minutes.

4. Why don't you ________________ more shop assistants during the summer?

(A) Most of the assistants ___________________.

(B) I think I'll ___________________.

(C) My assistant is on ______________________.

Technical Point

● 基本的な前置詞でも見落としやすい使い方を正しく理解しておく

例題 1（　）の中から正しい形を選びなさい。

Though Sally usually walks her dog (at / on / in) the morning, she stayed at home (at / on / in) the morning of October 12.

比較的長い期間の morning には in を使いますが，特定の日を述べる場合は on を使います。

● まぎらわしい前置詞は，特に文全体の意味を確認して選ぶ

例題 2（　）の中から正しい語を選びなさい。

Our client is supposed to come (by / until) 10 o'clock.

「10 時までに来ることになっている」という意味にするのが自然なので，期限を表す by を使います。until は「～まで」という意味で継続を表します。of「（材料）～で」と from「（原料）～から」や，beside「～のそばに」と besides「～に加えて」などにも注意しましょう。

● あとに続く語の特徴をつかみ，正しい前置詞を選ぶ

例題 3（　）の中から正しい語を選びなさい。

a) She has been working for the insurance company (for / during) seven years.

b) Mr. Wilson was in the hospital (for / during) the summer holidays.

a) の「7 年」のようにそれ自体で時間の長さを表す語が続く場合は for を選び「7 年間」とします。

b) の「夏休み」のように，特定の季節や出来事，時期などの語が続く場合は during を選び「夏休みの間」とします。

ほかに，between「（2 つのもの）の間」と among「（3 つ以上のもの）の間」，by「（行為者）によって」と with「（道具）で」なども，あとに続く語に注目して選ぶようにします。

● ディスコースマーカーを覚えて文選択の手がかりにする

PART 6 の空所に入れる文を選ぶ問題では，文と文を論理的につなげる語句（ディスコースマーカー）が手がかりになることがあります。例えば，空所に入る文に，furthermore（意味「そのうえ」）という，「追加」の役割を持つ語があれば，空所前の文に何か情報を加えているはずです。

よく使われるディスコースマーカーの意味と役割を確認しておきましょう。

「追加」moreover / furthermore / in addition

「例示」for example / for instance

「結果」so / therefore / thus

「逆接」but / however / nevertheless

「原因」because / as / since

Training for the TOEIC L&R Test

PART 6: Select the best answers to complete the text.
Questions 1-4 refer to the following letter.

Dear Friends:

Peace Pediatrics is proud to announce the addition of Dr. Karen White to our practice. Dr. White was born ------- **1.** April 10th, 1980, and raised just north of Maple City, attending Maple City public schools from kindergarten through 12th grade. She then studied Human Biology at Brown University, with a concentration in Disability as well as Child Development. Dr. White is a graduate of Harvard Medical School and worked with us here at Peace Pediatrics one day per week ------- **2.** her internship. ------- **3.**

Today, ------- **4.** being a fine physician, Dr. White is happily married and the proud mother of a baby boy. She looks forward to working with patients with a wide variety of medical needs. We feel very fortunate to introduce her to you as our new partner.

Sincerely,

Jim Wilson, MD   Martha Belcher, MD   Daniel Moore, MD

1. (A) in
(B) on
(C) at
(D) by

2. (A) at
(B) during
(C) for
(D) while

3. (A) So, some of you attended Maple City public schools.
(B) So, some of you may have already met her.
(C) So, she was interested in Human Biology.
(D) So, she is happy to announce the graduation of Brown University.

4. (A) beyond
(B) because
(C) beside
(D) besides

1. Ⓐ Ⓑ Ⓒ Ⓓ   **2.** Ⓐ Ⓑ Ⓒ Ⓓ   **3.** Ⓐ Ⓑ Ⓒ Ⓓ   **4.** Ⓐ Ⓑ Ⓒ Ⓓ

Reading Section　PART 7 説明文とレシピ

Technical Point ● レシピ特有の表現に慣れ，説明文の情報と合わせて料理を作るつもりで読む

レシピ (recipe) とは，料理の材料や調理法を記したものです。簡潔に書かれているので，語彙に慣れれば手順がすぐにわかるようになります。よく使われる調理用語として，小さじ 1 杯（1 teaspoon, 5 ml），大さじ 1 杯（1 tablespoon, 15 ml），カップ 1 杯（1 cup, 200 ml），みじん切り (mince)，角切り (cube)，かきまぜる (stir)，炒める (sauté)，とろ火で煮る (simmer) などがあります。食材については見慣れない語もある場合も考えられますが，意味が全てわからなくても問題を解けることが多いので，あまりこだわらないようにしましょう。レシピと説明文があるのは，両方を読まないと正確に調理ができない場合です。設問の中の条件が説明文に書いてあることと関連している場合は特に注意し，実際にその条件で調理の手順を追っていくつもりで答えを探しましょう。よく問われることは，出来上がりが何人前か，調理時間はどれくらいか，特殊な食材をどのように扱うか，などです。

● NOT 型設問では本文と一致しないものを選ぶ

PART 7 の設問の中には，「～でないもの」を問う NOT と大文字で書かれたものがあります。

・What is NOT included in XXX?　　・Which of the following is NOT true?

このような「NOT 型設問」に対しては，選択肢 1 つずつ本文と照合します。本文に書かれていたり，内容的に一致したりするものを外していき，残ったものが正解です。

Training for the TOEIC L&R Test

PART 7: Select the best answer to each question.
Questions 1-5 refer to the following instructions and recipe.

Enjoy Microwave Oven Cooking

Microwave cooking is a quick and easy way to prepare delicious, nutritious food. Once you've become familiar with your microwave oven, your work in the kitchen will be easier and more efficient. The recipes in this book are easy to follow and require mostly common ingredients available in any supermarket. So, whether you are a novice or an expert in the kitchen, your microwave oven will give you speedy and tasty results.

The ideal material for a microwave utensil allows energy to pass through the container and heat the food it contains. It must also be able to withstand contact with hot food or boiling liquids. You can use casserole dishes, or just look for materials that are marked "microwave-safe."

Food prepared in a microwave oven cooks from the outside toward the center. Thus, place the thicker part of all meats toward the outside edge of the dish.

Lids and plastic wrap provide steam and heat retention. Open a small vent at a corner when using plastic wrap to keep it from bursting. "Cover" in this book means cover with a microwave-safe lid or vented plastic wrap.

All the recipes in this book were tested in a 1000-watt microwave oven. If you have a lower wattage oven, you will need to increase the cooking time. For example, what cooks on 1000 watts for 3 minutes cooks on 500 watts for 6 minutes. Do not overcook. Always undercook and test to see if your dish is done. You can add more time as needed.

Recipe No. 25: Seasoned Drumsticks

[Makes 4 servings]

8 chicken drumsticks
1 tablespoon dried parsley flakes
1 teaspoon dried tarragon leaves
1/4 cup butter
2 teaspoons chopped chives
salt and pepper to taste

Place butter in a small bowl. Microwave in a 1000-watt oven about 1 minute, to melt. Stir in remaining ingredients except chicken, salt and pepper. Set aside. Place chicken drumsticks in a casserole. Brush with half of the butter mixture. Cover. Microwave about 7 minutes. Turn over and brush with remaining butter mixture. Microwave about 3 minutes. Serve with salt and pepper.

1. Who can enjoy microwave cooking?
(A) Only experts in using microwave ovens
(B) Only those who work in the kitchen most efficiently
(C) Both novices and experts in the kitchen
(D) Only those who have a 1000-watt microwave oven

2. Why can casserole dishes be used in a microwave oven?
(A) Because they allow microwaves to pass through them and heat the food.
(B) Because they have a vent in the corner.
(C) Because they can be covered with plastic wrap.
(D) Because they cook from the outside in.

3. What ingredients are included in the butter mixture besides butter?
(A) Drumsticks, parsley, tarragon leaves, and chives
(B) Parsley, tarragon leaves, and chives
(C) Parsley, tarragon leaves, chives, and pepper
(D) Tarragon leaves, chives, salt, and pepper

4. How long is the cooking time for the drumsticks in total if using a 500-watt microwave oven?
(A) About 5 minutes and 30 seconds
(B) About 11 minutes
(C) About 22 minutes
(D) About 44 minutes

5. Which of the following is NOT true?
(A) The thicker part of a piece of meat should be placed toward the outside edge of the dish.
(B) Undercooking is better than overcooking, as you can add more time if necessary.
(C) The drumsticks should be turned over after being cooked for about 7 minutes.
(D) With recipe No. 25, there is one drumstick per serving.

1. Ⓐ Ⓑ Ⓒ Ⓓ **2.** Ⓐ Ⓑ Ⓒ Ⓓ **3.** Ⓐ Ⓑ Ⓒ Ⓓ **4.** Ⓐ Ⓑ Ⓒ Ⓓ **5.** Ⓐ Ⓑ Ⓒ Ⓓ

Unit 15

PART 3 ビジネス会話

PART 5 不定詞の重要表現①

Listening Section　PART 3 ビジネス会話

Technical Point

● 最初の発話に集中し，場所・状況・2人の関係等の場面設定をつかむ

例題 会話を聞き，それに関する質問に対して最も適切なものを選びなさい。 64

What's wrong with the tie?

(A) It doesn't go with navy blue.

(B) It's too loud.

(C) It's too expensive.

(D) It's round at the tip.

Ⓐ Ⓑ Ⓒ Ⓓ

PART3 では最初の発話を聞き取ることができると場面設定をイメージしやすく，正答率が上がります。会話の場所と，男性・女性の関係に注意を向けて，空所を埋めながら会話文を完成させましょう。

W: Good morning, sir. 1.________________________ you?

M: Well, I'm looking for a tie to 2._________________ a navy blue blazer.

W: How about this one? This color goes very well with navy.

M: I'm afraid it's a little too 3.______________ for my taste.

まず，最初の発話 "Good morning, sir." からお店での会話だと推測できます。"May I help you?" はお店での定番表現として知られていますが，その他にも "Were/Are you looking for anything in particular?"「何かお探しですか？」("Were you ～" と過去形にすることで丁寧な表現となります) や "Let me know if you need anything."「何か必要なものがあればお知らせください」なども覚えておくと良いでしょう。

次に，男性が「紺のジャケットに合うネクタイを探している」と言っています。"look for ～"「～を探す」や "go with ～ "「～と合う」はよく使われる表現です。

その後，店員の女性は "How about ～?"「～はどうですか？」と提案していますが，男性は "too loud"「派手すぎる」と言っていることから (B) が正解だと判断できます。"How about ～?" は "What about ～?" と同様に「～はどうですか？」という意味です。ぜひ覚えておきましょう。

Training for the TOEIC L&R Test

PART 3: You will hear two short conversations. Select the best answer to each question.

65

1. What problem does the woman have?

(A) She can't reserve a room for the lunch meeting.
(B) She has left something behind at the corner of the room.
(C) She has to lift books to the rooftop of the café.
(D) She is not sure where the meeting will be held.

Ⓐ Ⓑ Ⓒ Ⓓ

2. Look at the graphic. Where does the man tell the woman to go?

(A) Room A
(B) Room B
(C) Room C
(D) Room D

Floor layout

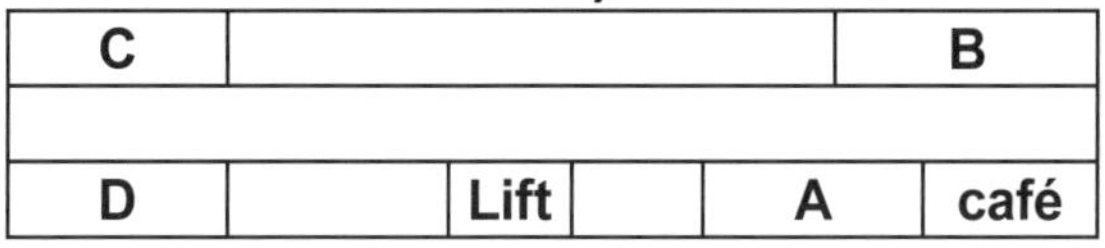

Ⓐ Ⓑ Ⓒ Ⓓ

3. What will the woman most likely do tomorrow?

(A) Find the room without big problems.
(B) Attend another meeting by herself.
(C) Eat lunch alone in the café.
(D) Bring a cake she will bake.

Ⓐ Ⓑ Ⓒ Ⓓ

66

4. What is the man going to do the day after tomorrow?

(A) He will meet a manager at another company.
(B) He will sign a contract with another company.
(C) He will talk about how their office should be changed.
(D) He will prepare some materials for a good meal.

Ⓐ Ⓑ Ⓒ Ⓓ

5. Look at the graphic. At what time will the man and woman have the Department meeting tomorrow?

(A) At 11:00.
(B) At 13:00
(C) At 14:00
(D) At 16:00

Yutaka's Time Table [Wednesday, June 9th]

Time	Events
9:00	Briefing
10:00	Meeting for the promotional campaign
11:00	
12:00	Lunch with Lars
13:00	
14:00	
15:00	Manager meeting
16:00	

Ⓐ Ⓑ Ⓒ Ⓓ

6. How will the woman let the members know the time for tomorrow's Department meeting ?

(A) She'll put up a notice.
(B) She'll ask her secretary.
(C) She'll send an email.
(D) She'll write a blog post.

Ⓐ Ⓑ Ⓒ Ⓓ

Partial Dictation

Questions 1-3

W: Jack, do you remember 1._______________ our lunch meeting will be held tomorrow?

M: Yeah, it's Room 802. It's not Room 206 that we usually use. Cathy said it had already been 2._______________ by another group.

W: I've never been there. Where is it?

M: It's on the top floor. The view from the room is really great! Take the lift to the top floor. When you get out of the lift, 3.____________________ and go straight. You'll find it 4.____________________________________ on the left, just 5.____________________ the Café.

W: Thanks. I think I can get there by myself now.

Questions 4-6

M: Hi. I got an appointment with the Sales Manager at P&Z company. I am seeing him the day after tomorrow.

W: Wow, Yutaka, that's great! Then, we'll have to fix 1.____ with them and 2._______________________ for a good deal before you see him. Can we schedule some time to talk about them tomorrow?

M: Well, tomorrow …. Is it possible to 3.__________________ the Department meeting from 10 to 4._______________ the Manager meeting?

W: Definitely. Seeing a person of importance at P&Z is far more important for our company. I'll 5._______________ all the members joining the Department meeting.

M: Thank you for your help.

Reading Section　PART 5　不定詞の重要表現 ①

Technical Point

● 名詞・形容詞・副詞として使われる不定詞

例題 1（　　）の中から正しい形を選びなさい。

a) I have work (to do / doing), so I can't go out with you now.

b) He came by (to see / for see) my mother.

c) This year we hope (sell / to sell) 1,100 cars.

d) It is difficult (for / of) me to find someone whom I can depend on.

e) It was so kind (for / of) him to help me.

to- 不定詞（to + 動詞の原形）は，名詞・形容詞・副詞と同じように扱うことができます。

a) は to do が work を修飾し，形容詞のようなはたらきをしています（形容詞的用法）。「するべき仕事」という意味です。

b) の to see は「会うために」という意味で，副詞としてはたらいています（副詞的用法）。

c) では「売ること」という意味になる不定詞を選びます（名詞的用法）。他には it is ... to- 不定詞のように，仮に it を使って表していたものを，to- 不定詞で受けることもあります。その場合，d) のように「…にとって」という意味を持つ for ... が挿入されることがありますが，[it is + 人の性質を表す形容詞 + to- 不定詞] の場合は，of が使われます (e)。人の性質を表す形容詞には，kind（親切な），smart/wise（賢い），stupid（愚かな）などがあげられます。

● 不定詞の否定表現や頻出熟語

例題 2（　　）の中から正しい形を選びなさい。

a) The teacher told him (study / to study / studying) harder.

b) She promised me (not to / to not / don't) do that again.

c) (Making / Make / To make) matters worse, it started to rain.

主語 + 動詞の後に to- 不定詞が使われることもよくあります。

a) は[tell + 人 + to- 不定詞]で「人に～するように言う」という意味です。同様の使い方に，expect（～することを期待する，してほしいと思う），advise（～するように勧める），ask（～するように頼む），allow（～することを許可する）などがあります。

（例）The committee expects him to write a letter of apology.
　　　My mother asked me to wash the dishes.

b) のように不定詞が否定語（not，never など）とともに使われる場合は，語順に注意が必要です。not/never + to の語順となります。

c) は to make matters worse で「さらに悪いことに」という意味の熟語です。他に to be honest/frank（正直に言うと），so to speak（言わば），needless to say（言うまでもないが）などの不定詞を伴う熟語表現がよく使用されます。

PART 5: Select the best answer to complete each sentence.

1. The staff members will be provided with ------- during the meeting.

(A) something drinking
(B) something to drink
(C) anything drinking
(D) anything to drink

2. The marketing manager makes it a rule ------- snacks in the office, since she believes that this would decrease work efficiency.

(A) never eat
(B) never to eat
(C) never eaten
(D) to eat

3. Eventually, all of us are forced ------- a conscious decision about how we choose to live our lives.

(A) make
(B) made
(C) making
(D) to make

4. He still found ------- difficult to explain why he had decided to study Business Administration in Australia.

(A) that
(B) it
(C) even
(D) being

5. Though the product manager had asked ------- submit the sales report as soon as possible, Jim simply forgot to do so.

(A) him
(B) him to
(C) to him
(D) his

1. Ⓐ Ⓑ Ⓒ Ⓓ **2.** Ⓐ Ⓑ Ⓒ Ⓓ **3.** Ⓐ Ⓑ Ⓒ Ⓓ **4.** Ⓐ Ⓑ Ⓒ Ⓓ **5.** Ⓐ Ⓑ Ⓒ Ⓓ

6. We did not know ------- about the price of timber, which happened to fall right after David Corporation had merged with Packard, Ltd.

(A) to do
(B) so as to do
(C) where to do
(D) what to do

7. The memo says that the president ------- make a speech to the employees this evening.

(A) is to
(B) be to
(C) is being
(D) will be

8. ------- fully comprehend the relationship between product development and consumer satisfaction, it is necessary to look at the empirical studies.

(A) So that
(B) In order to
(C) Because of
(D) Not to

9. The chief executive of East Airlines appears ------- in his attempt to convince the city council to approve his plan, even though he repeatedly pointed out its merits.

(A) to fall
(B) to have fallen
(C) to fail
(D) to have failed

10. The parents made it clear that they did not want their children ------- as subjects in laboratory experiments.

(A) to be treated
(B) to treated
(C) treating
(D) be treated

6. Ⓐ Ⓑ Ⓒ Ⓓ **7.** Ⓐ Ⓑ Ⓒ Ⓓ **8.** Ⓐ Ⓑ Ⓒ Ⓓ **9.** Ⓐ Ⓑ Ⓒ Ⓓ **10.** Ⓐ Ⓑ Ⓒ Ⓓ

Unit 16

PART 4 ガイドの説明

PART 6 不定詞の重要表現②

PART 7 社内文書

Listening Section　PART 4 ガイドの説明

Technical Point

● ガイドの説明は，話し手・聞き手・場所・順序に注意

ガイドの説明では，ツアーガイドや研修の案内などが放送されます。注意すべきは，話し手・聞き手・場所・順序です。話し手と聞き手が誰で，お互いどういう関係なのかを放送の前半でつかみ，その上で，アナウンスが行われている場所はどこかに注意を向けます。ツアー等で移動がある場合や，研修のプログラムなどは，順序を整理しながら聞きます。

例題 次のガイドを聞き，それに関する質問に対して最も適切なものを選びなさい。　67

What is the best way to tour Oxford?

(A) Walking

(B) Double-decker buses

(C) Taxi

(D) Punting

Ⓐ Ⓑ Ⓒ Ⓓ

例題では，話し手はツアーコンダクターで，聞き手はツアーの参加者であると推測できます。アナウンスが行われている場所は，観光地に到着する前のバスの車内等が考えられます。もう一度聞いて，下線部に語句を書き入れなさい。

We're very happy to have you join us on a tour of Oxford today. It's one of the most beautiful cities in Britain and is steeped in history and tradition. Oxford is a city best discovered 1.__________________. Traveling on foot is 2.____________ for exploring the sights, the city center and the famous colleges. We'll also take a pleasant 3.____________ along the river, where we may see rowing crews out practicing and some punters, too. There are a number of excellent pubs in Oxford, some of which are said to be as old as the famous colleges. We'll stop in for 4._________ at one of the oldest. Today's tour will last about 5.___________________, so let's be on our way.

設問ではガイドが勧める観光方法が問われています。選択肢とトランスクリプトの表現は同一ではありませんが，文脈から推測できるでしょう。正解は on foot，stroll ⇒ (A)Walking です。

Training for the TOEIC L&R Test

PART 4: You will hear two short talks. Select the best answer to each question.

68

1. What does the speaker mainly talk about?
(A) A program for starting an Internet business
(B) A program for basic business study skills
(C) A program for reporters and journalists
(D) A program for training teachers
Ⓐ Ⓑ Ⓒ Ⓓ

2. How long is the course?
(A) Two weeks
(B) Three weeks
(C) Eight weeks
(D) Ten weeks
Ⓐ Ⓑ Ⓒ Ⓓ

3. What are participants required to do to complete the course?
(A) Go to class and do their homework every day
(B) Take part in the introductory unit
(C) Be a successful business person
(D) Submit two essays and earn an overall pass grade
Ⓐ Ⓑ Ⓒ Ⓓ

69

4. Who is this message mainly for?
(A) Those who are planning to travel to England
(B) Those who are doing research on the weather in England
(C) Those who are interested in the geography in England
(D) Those who want to visit historical sites in England
Ⓐ Ⓑ Ⓒ Ⓓ

5. Which season is the most popular for tourists to visit England, according to the speaker?
(A) Spring
(B) Summer
(C) Autumn
(D) Winter
Ⓐ Ⓑ Ⓒ Ⓓ

6. Which is the best place to visit, according to the speaker?
(A) London, for its culture
(B) The South, for its beaches
(C) The North, for its history
(D) It depends on what travelers are interested in.
Ⓐ Ⓑ Ⓒ Ⓓ

Partial Dictation

Questions 1-3

Hi, everyone. I'm Hisako Taylor. Today I'll be briefing you about our program for basic 1.______________________________. The course consists of 2.______________ focusing on the following skills: Reading, Note-taking and Basic Report Writing. There is also an introductory unit outlining the content of the course and explaining the online mode of study. The course draws material from many business situations. It is interactive and provides regular opportunities for you to practice the study skills covered in a variety of activities and exercises. Each unit will require up to ten hours' study time spread over a 3.______________ period. The duration of the course is 4.______________. In order to complete the course successfully you will be required to submit 5______________________ and achieve an overall 6.______________.

Questions 4-6

Thank you for your enquiries about England. Here are 1.______________ to three of your questions. First, "Which is the best time of year to visit?" Well, high season is from June until around the end of August. This is the 2.______________________________________, when accommodation is most expensive. So you might save a few pounds if you do not mind traveling in the off-season. But keep in mind that some attractions are closed then. Second, "Is the weather really that bad?" Tourists often talk about how bad the weather in England is, but it all depends on the time of 3.______________________________. In summer it can be very 4.____________________ the rest of Europe. In winter it can be very pleasant, as well. As most people say, 5.________________ is all part of the charm. Take it as a part of England. Third, "Which is the best location to visit?" There is no easy answer to this question. It all depends on the 6.______________ of holiday you wish to have and what you are trying to get out of your trip to England. London is great for a big cultural, historical city experience, the South for a coastal holiday, and the North for historical significance.

Reading Section　PART 6　不定詞の重要表現 ②

Technical Point

● 使役動詞や知覚動詞とともに使われる動詞の形に注意

例題（　　）の中から正しい形を選びなさい。

a) My mother made me (come / came / coming) home before 9 P.M. when I was young.

b) Let me (buy / to buy) you a cup of coffee.

c) He got the new secretary (copy / to copy) the document.

d) The owner of the hotel had the lobby (to redecorate / redecorated).

e) I saw the man (break / broke) into my house.

「～させる」という意味合いを持つ動詞を「使役動詞」と言い，使役動詞とともに原形不定詞（動詞の原形）を用いることがあります。

・make + 目的語 + 動詞の原形「～させる」
He made me go to school. 彼は私を学校に行かせた。

・let + 目的語 + 動詞の原形「望むように～させる」
I let him use my car. 彼に私の車を使わせた。

・have + 目的語 + 動詞の原形「～してもらう」,「～させる」
I had my father repair my car. 父に車を修理してもらった。

・get + 目的語 + to + 動詞の原形「～させる」という意味のgetにはto-不定詞 (to + 動詞の原形) を用います。
I got Jim to review the report. ジムに報告書を吟味させた。(例題 c)

* 目的語が動作を受ける場合は使役動詞 + 目的語 + 過去分詞となります。(例題 d)
I had my car repaired by my father.
I got the report reviewed by Jim.

「～が…するのを見る，聞く，感じる」という意味で see, look at, hear, listen to, feel などとともに動詞の原形が使われます（例題 e)。
この場合，動詞の原形ではなく，現在分詞 (...ing) を用いることもあります。

I saw the man breaking into my house. 私はその男が私の家に侵入するところを見た。

ただし，このような文を受動態にする場合は to が必要となります。

The man was seen to break into my house. その男は私の家に侵入するのを見られた。

Training for the TOEIC L&R Test

PART 6: Select the best answers to complete the text.
Questions 1-4 refer to the following article.

> Kathy,
>
> Thanks for your comments regarding the class. It was very nice ------- **1.** you to take the time to give me your feedback. I'm glad you are getting so much from the course. I have to agree with you that it's wonderful watching presentations. I too learn so much and feel so lucky that I can be a part of students' learning experiences, especially as presentations seem ------- **2.** so many interesting aspects of individual students. I hope watching the presentations of peers has made students ------- **3.** upon their own presentations. As I've written on the evaluation sheet, yours was especially great. ------- **4.** I really hope you do more. Have a great weekend, too.
>
> John

1. (A) by
(B) for
(C) of
(D) to

2. (A) to demonstrate
(B) demonstrated
(C) demonstrating
(D) demonstrate

3. (A) to reflect
(B) reflected
(C) reflecting
(D) reflect

4. (A) One of the most important aspects of presentation is how you deliver the message.
(B) When I heard you speak, I felt that you have a lot of important presentation skills and personal attributes that make you a terrific speaker.
(C) I would like to add that the course focuses on how to use presentation tools, rather than the delivery.
(D) I'm afraid that I have to decline your request to audit the class.

---

1. Ⓐ Ⓑ Ⓒ Ⓓ **2.** Ⓐ Ⓑ Ⓒ Ⓓ **3.** Ⓐ Ⓑ Ⓒ Ⓓ **4.** Ⓐ Ⓑ Ⓒ Ⓓ

Reading Section　PART 7　社内文書

Technical Point ● Re や Subject をチェックし，要旨を把握する

社内で情報を共有する際，E-mail による memo が社員宛に送信されることがよくあります。ここでいう memo とは，日本語の「メモ書き」などの意味とは多少異なり，「社内向けのちょっとしたお知らせ」のようなものです。差出人は human resources（人事部）や president（社長）など，宛て先は all employees，staff（従業員）などの場合があります。また，RE や Subject（件名）などの語の後に「何に関するお知らせか」が明記されている場合は，必ずそれをチェックしましょう。メモのポイントとなる語が使われていることが多く，内容を読みとる際のヒントとなります。

Training for the TOEIC L&R Test

PART 7: Select the best answer to each question.
Questions 1-3 refer to the following notice.

To:	**Department Managers**
From:	**Heidi Nueroth**
Re:	**Department Head Meeting**
Date:	**May 10**

The Department Head Meeting is set for May 20 in conference room 102, 10:00 A.M.-2:30 P.M. We will discuss our new product lines for the next spring season. Each department is encouraged to bring ideas for new products. Please discuss this with the members of your team beforehand. Lunch will be provided during the meeting as usual. If you are not able to attend, let me know in advance. In that case, you should submit your department's ideas to me via an email no later than a day before the scheduled meeting time.

1. What should managers bring to the meeting?
(A) Lunch
(B) Plans for future products
(C) Sales reports
(D) New products　Ⓐ Ⓑ Ⓒ Ⓓ

2. What should managers do if they cannot attend the meeting?
(A) Send an e-mail to Ms. Nueroth
(B) Reschedule the meeting
(C) Talk about new products with Ms. Nueroth in person
(D) Encourage their colleagues to attend the meeting instead　Ⓐ Ⓑ Ⓒ Ⓓ

3. What should managers do before attending the meeting?
(A) Purchase something to eat
(B) Send an e-mail to Ms. Nueroth
(C) Consult with other managers
(D) Discuss new product ideas with their staff　Ⓐ Ⓑ Ⓒ Ⓓ

Unit 17

PART 1 風景写真・人物と背景写真の描写

PART 5 条件と仮定法の表現 ①

Listening Section　PART 1 風景写真・人物と背景写真の描写

Technical Point

● 風景写真は全てが対象となる

例題 1 次の写真を最も適切に描写している英文を選びなさい。 70

Ⓐ Ⓑ Ⓒ Ⓓ

下線部に聞きとった語句を書きなさい。

(A) Some ________________ are swimming in the lake.

(B) There are some ________________ around the lake.

(C) ________________________ are flying over the lake.

(D) There are some ________________ on the lake.

風景写真で，例題 1 のように特に目立った対象がない場合は，全体と細部両方に気を配ります。人や飛んでいる鳥，また船は写っていませんので，木の描写が正解です。

● 人物だけでなく背景描写も聞き逃さないように

例題 2 次の写真を最も適切に描写している英文を選びなさい。 71

Ⓐ Ⓑ Ⓒ Ⓓ

下線部に聞きとった語句を書きなさい。

(A) The man is ________________ up the boxes.

(B) The man is ________________ the bottle to the cash register.

(C) The man is putting things into his ________________________.

(D) A lot of boxes are ________________ on the shelves.

例題 2 のように人物が写っていると，まずその人の動作の描写を予想しますが，the man から始まる描写はいずれも正しくありません。背景の 1 つである積み上げられた箱の描写が正解です。このように，写真の中心となる人物ではなく背景の一部の描写を正解とする場合があるので，聞き逃さないように注意が必要です。

Training for the TOEIC L&R Test

PART 1: Select the sentence that best describes what you see in each picture.

1. 72

Ⓐ Ⓑ Ⓒ Ⓓ

2. 73

Ⓐ Ⓑ Ⓒ Ⓓ

3. 74

Ⓐ Ⓑ Ⓒ Ⓓ

Partial Dictation

1. (A) Some of the people are ______________________________ the lake.

(B) There is ______________________________ on the lake.

(C) They are watching the boat ______________________________.

(D) There is ______________________________ across the lake.

2. (A) There are trees and bushes on ______________________________ of the road.

(B) There is no ______________________________ beside the road.

(C) The ______________________________ tracks go through the forest.

(D) The highway is ______________________________ with asphalt.

3. (A) The man is carrying a ______________________________.

(B) The man is ______________________________ the ladder.

(C) Some cars are ______________________________ in front of the building.

(D) The man is ______________________________ the station wagon.

Reading Section　PART 5 条件と仮定法の表現 ①

Technical Point

● 仮定法では，心理的な「距離感」を表すため「動詞の時制を１つずらす」

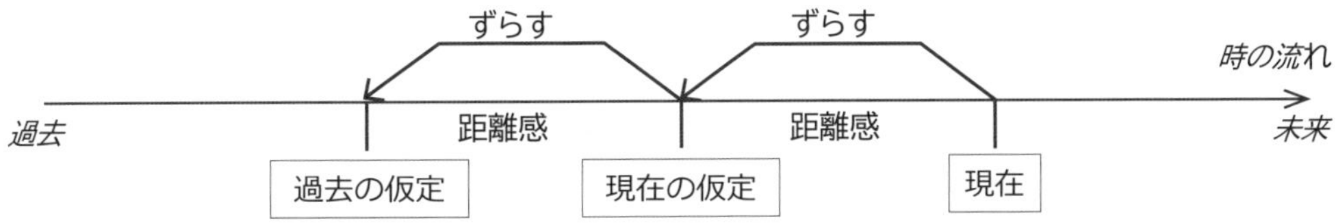

had 過去分詞	←	過去形	←	現在形
would /could /might + have 過去分詞	←	助動詞過去形	←	助動詞

（大西泰斗＆ポール・マクベイ，2005『ネイティブスピーカーの英文法絶対基礎力』研究社より引用）

● 現在の仮定：仮定法では，「現実との距離感」を表すため「動詞の時制を１つずらす」

例題（　　）の中から正しい形を選びなさい。

a)　If I (am / were / has been / had been) you, I would sign the contract.

英語では，現在形は「現在」と「現実」を表します。過去形は「過去」と「現実との距離感」を表す場合に使われます。

a) で仮に If I am you, I will sign the contract. とした場合，話し手は「私が君であるなら」「契約を結ぶ」という内容を「現実」的と捉えて話していることになります。しかし，ここでは後半の “would sign” から分かる通り，「私が君である」ことと「私が契約を結ぶ」ことはありえないと考えており，「現実とは距離を置いた仮定の話」=「仮定法」で表現しています。現在の話を仮定法で表現したい時は「現実との距離感」を持たせるため，それぞれの節の動詞の時制を「現在形から過去形へ」ずらします。仮定法の基本は「時制をずらす」です。基本的に「if ＋ S ＋ 過去形」＋「S ＋ 助動詞過去形 ＋ 動詞の原形」で現在の仮定です。

“If I am you, I will sign the contract.”
→ “If I were (was) you, I would sign the contract.”（主語が単数の場合 was も可能）

● 過去の仮定：仮定法では「過去の事実との距離感」を表すため「動詞の時制を１つずらす」

b)　If he (knows / knew / has known / had known) the market well then, he could have solved the problem.

b) も a) 同様に仮定法で，「動詞の時制をずらす」ことがポイントです。ただし b) には “then” や “could have solved” という過去を表す語句があることから過去の話だと判断できます。過去の話では「If 節内は had ＋ 過去分詞へ」「主節内は助動詞の過去形 ＋ have ＋ 過去分詞へ」時制をずらします。基本的に「if ＋ S ＋ had ＋ 過去分詞」＋「S ＋ 助動詞過去形 ＋ have ＋ 過去分詞」で過去の仮定です。

“If he knew the market well then, he could solve the problem.”
→ “If he had known the market well then, he could have solved the problem.”

Training for the TOEIC L&R Test

PART 5: Select the best answer to complete each sentence.

1. If I ------- better computer skills, it wouldn't take me so long to finish this report.

(A) have
(B) had
(C) have had
(D) had had

2. Our boss wouldn't have let us invest in the bond if he ------- the updated data.

(A) has
(B) had
(C) has had
(D) had had

3. If the current political situation in the country were better, it ------- more investments from abroad.

(A) attract
(B) attracts
(C) can attract
(D) could attract

4. If we had investigated the cause of the trouble more carefully, we ------- yesterday's trouble.

(A) avoided
(B) could avoid
(C) could have avoided
(D) had avoided

5. If I ------- in your shoes, I would accept the offer.

(A) am
(B) were
(C) have been
(D) be

1. Ⓐ Ⓑ Ⓒ Ⓓ **2.** Ⓐ Ⓑ Ⓒ Ⓓ **3.** Ⓐ Ⓑ Ⓒ Ⓓ **4.** Ⓐ Ⓑ Ⓒ Ⓓ **5.** Ⓐ Ⓑ Ⓒ Ⓓ

6. If you ------- the products at least three days earlier, we might have received them by the end of last month.

(A) ship
(B) shipped
(C) has shipped
(D) had shipped

7. If there ------- last-minute changes in the timetable, the symposium would have ended at the scheduled time.

(A) is not
(B) were not
(C) has not been
(D) had not been

8. His presentation might have been more polished ------- he had taken his manager's advice.

(A) if
(B) while
(C) unless
(D) whether

9. I wish I ------- French, because next week I'm meeting some important French executives.

(A) speak
(B) can speak
(C) could speak
(D) could have spoken

10. Since his job involves a lot of data analysis, he wishes he ------- statistics before he joined the company.

(A) studies
(B) studied
(C) has studied
(D) had studied

6. Ⓐ Ⓑ Ⓒ Ⓓ **7.** Ⓐ Ⓑ Ⓒ Ⓓ **8.** Ⓐ Ⓑ Ⓒ Ⓓ **9.** Ⓐ Ⓑ Ⓒ Ⓓ **10.** Ⓐ Ⓑ Ⓒ Ⓓ

Unit 18

PART 2 特殊な疑問文にすばやく反応する

PART 6 条件と仮定法の表現②

PART 7 トリプルパッセージの問題

Listening Section　PART 2 特殊な疑問文にすばやく反応する

Technical Point

● 付加疑問文は付加を，否定疑問文は否定をはずして内容に反応する

例題 1 問いかけの文に対し応答として最も適切な英文を選びなさい。
下線部に聞きとった語句を書きなさい。　75

She's a new sales clerk, isn't she?

(A) No, she ____________.

(B) Yes, she _______.

(C) No, ________________.

Ⓐ Ⓑ Ⓒ

例題 1 は付加疑問文で「彼女は新しい販売員ですね」と相手に確認するときに使います。答える側は「販売員である」と思えば Yes, そうでなければ No, のようにあくまでも内容に反応するように答えます。例題 1 では時制や主語に注意し，(B) を選びます。

例題 2 問いかけの文に対し応答として最も適切な英文を選びなさい。
下線部に聞きとった語句を書きなさい。　76

Wasn't he a plant manager before?

(A) Yes, he _______ a manager.

(B) No, he doesn't have _________________.

(C) __________ sure.

Ⓐ Ⓑ Ⓒ

例題 2 のような否定疑問文にすばやく反応するには，否定語を切り離して「彼は工場長でした。そうではありませんでしたか」と意味をとり，「～ではありませんでした」の部分を気にせずに，内容に同意できれば Yes, そうでなければ No, と答えます。(A) は時制が違い，(B) は関係ない内容なので，「わからない」の（C）が正解です。Yes/No 疑問文の応答が Yes，No のから始まるとは限らない，というポイントも活用します（Unit 2 参照）。

例題 1 の文について，付加された isn't she をはずし，また例題 2 の文については否定 not をはずしてそれぞれ Yes/No 疑問文にしてみましょう。

例題 1. Is she a new sales clerk?	Yes，she is.
例題 2. Was he a plant manager before?	I'm not sure.

応答はそれぞれの正解と同じで差し支えないことがわかります。このように，付加疑問文は付加を，否定疑問文は否定を気にせず，内容に集中すると速く解くことができます。

Training for the TOEIC L&R Test

PART 2: You will hear four questions and three possible responses to each. Select the best response to each question.

77-80

1. Ⓐ Ⓑ Ⓒ　　**2.** Ⓐ Ⓑ Ⓒ

3. Ⓐ Ⓑ Ⓒ　　**4.** Ⓐ Ⓑ Ⓒ

Partial Dictation

1. You know how to ________________ Mr. Wells, don't you?

(A) Yes, he and I are ________________ touch.

(B) Yes, I have his __________________________.

(C) Yes, he ________________ the contract.

2. ________________ supposed to make a speech last Friday?

(A) The speech was ________________.

(B) I ________________.

(C) Yes, but ___________________ came up.

3. You've already opened a ________________ at this bank, haven't you?

(A) Yes, I ________________ into account.

(B) Yes, the bank is ___________________ 5 o'clock.

(C) Yes, but there's ___________________ in it.

4. ________________ install the new software program?

(A) I ________________.

(B) Yes, ________________ right away.

(C) No, the program is ________________ begin.

Reading Section　PART 6 条件と仮定法の表現 ②

Technical Point

● 条件節：「現実にありえる」と話し手が思っている場合 --- if 節内でも時制をずらさない

例題（　）の中から正しい形を選びなさい。

a) If this (be / is / were / had been) the case, we have to stop dealing with them.

b) If he (be / is / was / had been) on the bullet train, he was probably admiring its speed and comfort.

if 節内であっても, 話し手が「現実にありえる」と思っていれば時制をずらさずに, 現在の話なら現在形, 過去の話なら過去形を用います。

a) では主節内の "have to" から, 仮定法ではないと判断できるため（仮定法であれば, " 助動詞の過去形 + 原形 " であるはず）, 現在形の is を選びます。

b) では, 主節内の "was" から仮定法ではないと判断できるため（仮定法であれば, 過去の仮定を表す " 助動詞の過去形 + have + 過去分詞 " であるはず）, 過去形の was を選びます。b) の意味は「（乗ったかどうかわからないが）彼が新幹線に乗っていたら, おそらくそのスピードと快適さを称賛していたであろう。」となります。

● これから現実にしたいが , まだ現実になっていない仮定 --- 時制を持たない「原形」を使う

例題（　）の中から正しい形を選びなさい。

c) They required that she (show / shows / showed / has shown) her ID.

d) It is necessary that any candidate (be / is / was / has been) qualified for the post.

「これから現実にしたいが, まだ現実になっていないこと」を表す場合,「動詞の原形」を使います。なぜなら, どの時点においてもまだ現実になっていないものは, 時を確定する現在形や過去形といった「時制」を持つことができないからです。

c) のように何かを要求する（require）場合,「要求する内容（that 以下）」は「まだ現実になっていない仮定」であるため, 時制を持つことができません。ちなみに, 命令文に原形が使われるのも同じ理由からです。

d) も that 以下の「必要な内容」は「まだ現実になっていない仮定」のため, 時制を持つことができません。このように要求・主張・提案を表す動詞（require, request, recommend, demand, insist, suggest 等）や必要性を表す形容詞（necessary, essential, desirable, imperative 等）に続く that 節内の動詞は原形（もしくは should + 原形）を用います。

（大西泰斗＆ポール・マクベイ, 2005『ネイティブスピーカーの英文法絶対基礎力』研究社）

Training for the TOEIC L&R Test

PART 6: Select the best answers to complete the text.
Questions 1-4 refer to the following letter.

JOB OPPORTUNITY

Taishi & Ambition Design Company is inviting applications for the positions of Web designers. It is desirable that applicants ------- **1.** more than 2 years' Web-design experience. The successful candidates will work in a group of eight to ten for the first month. ------- **2.** Through working with various people, you will get used to communicating with our staff members and will also be trained in the special skills we have developed. We would like to see what your strong points are. Even if you ------- **3** excellent at some work, we could offer you a different job.

Spending time with diverse team members will enable you to fit in well with our company. We are friendly and open-minded.

If you ------- **4.** interested in working with us, please download the application form from https://www.taishi&ambition.com and send us your CV along with your portfolio by July 25.

1. (A) had
(B) have
(C) will have
(D) would have

2. (A) The candidates are required to design a Web page on their own in this group.
(B) The candidates can use a PC and all the tools available in the section.
(C) We will test their skills in Web designing at the beginning of the period.
(D) The members of this group range from young to seasoned designers.

3. (A) can't be
(B) aren' t
(C) weren't
(D) haven't been

4. (A) are
(B) were
(C) had been
(D) be

1. Ⓐ Ⓑ Ⓒ Ⓓ **2.** Ⓐ Ⓑ Ⓒ Ⓓ **3.** Ⓐ Ⓑ Ⓒ Ⓓ **4.** Ⓐ Ⓑ Ⓒ Ⓓ

Reading Section PART 7 トリプルパッセージの問題

Technical Point

トリプルパッセージでは，3つの文書を読んで5つの設問を解きます。まずは1つめの文書をよく読み，ビジネスの内容をつかむことが大切です。また，メール・広告・記事等の文書にはそれぞれ「それを作った目的・狙い」があることも忘れないでください。「このメール（広告・記事等）の目的・狙いは何か」を考えながら読むことが正答を導くコツです。なかには3つの文書から正答を推測させる問題もありますが，文書内の情報を結び付ければ必ず解答できます。落ち着いて取り組みましょう。

PART 7: Select the best answer to each question.
Questions 1-5 refer to the following advertisement, e-mail, and Web page.

MIE City Council Workshop Schedule
All activities are 1 term long. In each term you have 4 lessons.

Activity and Instructor	Day	Description
Explorers Conducted by Stephan Gale	Monday	Join Explorers to discuss stimulating issues, do your own research, and create a written work. £30 per month
Art Makers Conducted by Joanna Levene	Tuesday	Art Makers will broaden your view of Art! Discover various ways of making art. £20 per month
Young Crafters Conducted by Sayako Somerville	Wednesday	Sign up for Young Crafters. Make your own original craft objects. Suitable for young children. £40 per month (clay and woodwork included)
British Chefs Conducted by Edward McKay	Thursday	British Chefs will show how to cook the traditional cuisine of England, Wales, Scotland and Northern Ireland. £20 per lesson (ingredients included)

*To book or for details, please e-mail us at staff@miecitycouncil.com.
*Participants are required to sign up 2 weeks before their first lesson day at the latest.
*10% concession when booked 2 months in advance.

To:	**Service Staff < miestaff@miecitycouncil.com>**
From:	**mcharlotte@tamail.com**
Re:	**Enquiries**
Date:	**22 April**

To Whom It May Concern,

Hello. I am interested in British Chefs in the workshops. But before I sign up, I would like to know about the following two points.
First, the course fee for British Chefs is "per lesson" while those for the other courses are "per month." Is this a typo? If it's not, why is it so expensive compared to the others?

Second, if possible, could you tell me Edward's career background? I'm eager to know how he has become able to instruct some good ways to cook the cuisines of all the four countries in the U.K.

I would appreciate it if you could give me a reply as soon as possible.

Best regards,
Charlotte Miller

http://www.miecitycouncil.org

MIE City Council

Exhibitions | Tea & Talks | Workshops | **Reviews** | Booking

Edward's British Chefs is great! Before I signed up, I was wondering if anyone could really tell us how to cook all kinds of cuisine in the four countries in the U.K. No worries. Edward has a deep understanding of each cooking style of the four countries. I will copy his background information below, which is now uploaded on the City Council Web site. The way he instructed was awesome. He lectured about some basic history of each cuisine, which enabled us to understand why we use the ingredients and why we cook them that way and so on. He sometimes told jokes to try and relax us and showed us how we should wash, cut, or cook the ingredients right before our eyes.
I strongly recommend this workshop to you all!
By the way, this course fee was 20 pounds "per lesson" not "per month" because this included all the food materials and use of tools. So I don't think this fee is high. Hope this is of help to those considering signing up!

— Charlotte Miller

Edward was brought up in Scotland and Northern Ireland enjoying their traditional home cuisines. Then he went on to the London School of Culinary Arts where he learned a high degree of skill in cooking and culinary art. After graduating, he started his career at a friendly bistro in Cardiff, worked for a five-star restaurant in Birmingham, and became the head chef at a first-class hotel in London.

1. What does the advertisement suggest about the workshops?
(A) Some discounts are available for local elderly people.
(B) Dropping in on the day without a reservation is not accepted.
(C) People aged 18 or over cannot join Young Crafters.
(D) Each activity has only one lesson in one term. Ⓐ Ⓑ Ⓒ Ⓓ

2. What is the purpose of the e-mail?
(A) To get detailed information about the fee and the instructor
(B) To receive discounts on the course fee for British Chefs
(C) To check if there is room in British Chefs and get a place in it
(D) To cancel the appointment the sender made in advance Ⓐ Ⓑ Ⓒ Ⓓ

3. In the e-mail, the word "typo" in paragraph 2 in line 2 is closest in meaning to
(A) an imprint
(B) a reprint
(C) a sprint
(D) a misprint Ⓐ Ⓑ Ⓒ Ⓓ

4. What is most likely true about the reply from City Council to Charlotte Miller?
(A) It offered a place of the activity Charlotte applied for.
(B) It included explanation about the City Council policy.
(C) It had some information about Edward's CV.
(D) It kindly turned down Charlotte's request. Ⓐ Ⓑ Ⓒ Ⓓ

5. What does the review indicate about British Chefs?
(A) The instructor was well qualified and satisfactory.
(B) The content of the lessons was monotonous.
(C) The ingredients used for the course were fantastic.
(D) The participants were friendly and told funny jokes. Ⓐ Ⓑ Ⓒ Ⓓ

Unit 19

PART 3 オフィス内の会話

PART 5 疑問詞・関係詞・接続詞

Listening Section　PART 3　オフィス内の会話

Technical Point

● ビジネス用語とオフィス内で交わされる話題に慣れよう

例題 会話を聞き，それに関する質問に対して最も適切なものを選びなさい。 81

1. What does the woman say about the deal?

(A) It was postponed.
(B) It didn’t work out.
(C) It was a success.
(D) It was cancelled.

Ⓐ Ⓑ Ⓒ Ⓓ

2. When was the deal being negotiated?

(A) Three days ago
(B) The day before yesterday
(C) This afternoon
(D) This morning

Ⓐ Ⓑ Ⓒ Ⓓ

Part 3では会話の状況を素早く把握することが要求されるので，会話の音声が始まる前に質問文に目を通しておくほうがよいでしょう。オフィス内の会話ではCEO（最高経営責任者）COO（最高執行責任者）executive（管理職）などの役職名やdeal（取引），negotiation（交渉），sales/production quota（販売/生産ノルマ），commission（手数料），supplier（納入業者），growth rate（成長率），shipment（出荷，出荷品），board（役員会），product development（製品開発）training session（研修）などのビジネス用語が使われることがあります。また，オフィス内で交わされる話題は人事採用や異動，社内会議，機器のトラブルなどさまざまです。語彙や話題に慣れるとともに，会話全体の流れをつかむように聞きとっていきましょう。

例題では，問1は女性の最初の発話を言い換えている文が答えです。また問2のように特定の数値，時間，地名，商品など具体的な情報が問われていたら，会話を聞きながらそれらをしっかり記憶しておく必要があります。もう一度聞いて，会話を完成させてみましょう。

M: Were you successful with 1.________________ you were 2.______________________ ________?
W: No. It 3.______________________.
M: What was the problem?
W: We couldn’t 4.____________________________.

Training for the TOEIC L&R Test

PART 3: You will hear two short conversations. Select the best answer to each question.

82

1. Where did the conversation probably take place?
(A) In a factory
(B) In an office
(C) In Europe
(D) In a warehouse
Ⓐ Ⓑ Ⓒ Ⓓ

2. What does the woman say about her company's products?
(A) They are low-priced.
(B) They are high-priced.
(C) They are high-quality.
(D) They are selling well in America.
Ⓐ Ⓑ Ⓒ Ⓓ

3. Why is the company launching their new products in Europe?
(A) They have so many competitors in the domestic market.
(B) They have few competitors in the domestic market.
(C) They already have so many customers in Europe.
(D) They already know the European market very well.
Ⓐ Ⓑ Ⓒ Ⓓ

83

4. What happened to the speakers this month?
(A) They attracted a new customer.
(B) They found a good bargain.
(C) They couldn't meet their sales quota.
(D) They started a new business.
Ⓐ Ⓑ Ⓒ Ⓓ

5. How did they try to raise money?
(A) From new customers
(B) By increasing sales
(C) By attracting outside investors
(D) By offering discounts
Ⓐ Ⓑ Ⓒ Ⓓ

6. What do the speakers plan to do now?
(A) Go to Asia
(B) Implement a new plan
(C) Decide what went wrong
(D) Find the customer they lost
Ⓐ Ⓑ Ⓒ Ⓓ

Partial Dictation

Questions 1-3

M: What is your company's latest 1.________________________?

W: Our products are of 2.________________________, but we have so 3.____________________ here in America that we have recently 4.____________ our new products into the European market.

M: How's 5.______________________________ going?

W: Right now, we're 6.____ in order to decide 7.______________ to sell our products there.

Questions 4-6

M: So many things 1.____________________ all at once this past month.

W: I know. Not only did we fail to 2._________________________________, but we also 3.________________________________ customer into the bargain.

M: And we 4.______________________________________ from outside investors to 5._______________ our new business in Asia.

W: We have to effectively 6.___________________ our new marketing plan. That's the only way we can 7.______________________________ this difficult situation.

Reading Section　PART 5 疑問詞・関係詞・接続詞

Technical Point

● 文中の疑問詞

例題 1（　　）の中から正しい形を選びなさい。

I need to find out (that / when) the meeting starts.

上の例題の（　　）以下は find out の目的語となります。find out の目的語が that + S + V「～ということ」か when + S + V「いつ～するか」のどちらがよいかということになります。上の場合，「私はいつ会議が始まるかを知る必要がある。」という意味が適切なのでその意味になるものを選びます。なお，文中に疑問文が入る間接疑問文の場合，通常の疑問文を作るときに用いた do，does，did は省いて，例文のように「疑問詞 + S + V」の語順となります。この場合の V は例題のように人称，時制の制約を受けるので注意します。

[Quiz]（　　）の中から正しい形を選びなさい。

(1) I don't know (how / who) is responsible for the delay of the shipment.

(2) Show me (how / which) the new copier works.

● 関係詞

例題 2（　　）の中から正しい形を選びなさい。

We landed in Honolulu, (which / where) the sales convention took place.

例題の関係詞節 the sales convention took place と先行詞の Honolulu とは，前置詞 in/at がないと関連づけることが出来ません。このような場合は「前置詞 + which」か「関係副詞（where, when，why など）」が先行詞と関係詞節の間に入ります。

[Quiz]（　　）の中から正しい形を選びなさい。

(1) We landed in Honolulu, (which / where) has many big convention centers.

(2) A good rest is (what / that) you need most.

● 接続詞

例題 3（　　）の中から正しい形を選びなさい。

She was not aware of the fact (that / which) the company's growth rate was only 2% last year.

接続詞 that が名詞の直後に置かれてその名詞の内容を説明する場合があります。よく使われる名詞は knowledge，fact，information，idea，report，proof，conclusion などで，そのあとの that は「～という」という意味になります。

[Quiz]（　　）の中から正しい形を選びなさい。

(1) What surprised us was (that / if) he finally convinced the CEO to approve his project.

(2) They ignored the report (that / which) the region has a good market for their products.

Training for the TOEIC L&R Test

PART 5: Select the best answer to complete each sentence.

1. ------- is true of most big baseball games, tickets for tomorrow night's game against the Buffaloes are sold out.

(A) That
(B) As
(C) What
(D) Which

2. We distributed the folders in ------- you will find the area map, application card, and meal coupon for lunch.

(A) what
(B) which
(C) who
(D) that

3. We received the information ------- our supplier hasn't delivered the product yet.

(A) what
(B) which
(C) who
(D) that

4. Do you happen to know ------- is offering a workshop on effective protection against M&A?

(A) what
(B) which
(C) who
(D) that

5. Tell me ------- information you have on our competitor's new product.

(A) whatever
(B) whichever
(C) whoever
(D) however

---

1. Ⓐ Ⓑ Ⓒ Ⓓ **2.** Ⓐ Ⓑ Ⓒ Ⓓ **3.** Ⓐ Ⓑ Ⓒ Ⓓ **4.** Ⓐ Ⓑ Ⓒ Ⓓ **5.** Ⓐ Ⓑ Ⓒ Ⓓ

6. We seldom see our supervisors, ------- usually work in another office.

(A) what
(B) which
(C) who
(D) that

7. It was Liza Walter ------- did a product demonstration at this morning's marketing meeting.

(A) what
(B) which
(C) who
(D) as

8. You should take the two types of tablets, both of ------- are for your allergy, three times a day after meals.

(A) what
(B) which
(C) who
(D) that

9. Tell him ------- all ABC Air Lines flights that fit his schedule are booked up solid.

(A) what
(B) which
(C) who
(D) that

10. ------- course you choose, the tour will take most of the afternoon.

(A) Wherever
(B) Whenever
(C) Whichever
(D) However

6. Ⓐ Ⓑ Ⓒ Ⓓ **7.** Ⓐ Ⓑ Ⓒ Ⓓ **8.** Ⓐ Ⓑ Ⓒ Ⓓ **9.** Ⓐ Ⓑ Ⓒ Ⓓ **10.** Ⓐ Ⓑ Ⓒ Ⓓ

Unit 20

PART 4 ニュース

PART 6 気をつけたい助動詞の用法

PART 7 製品などの説明書

Listing Section　PART 4 ニュース

Technical Point ● 最初の文を聞き逃さないようにすることが大切

ニュースでは主内容について質問されます。文頭にトピックが示されるため最初の文に注意を払います。天気予報では過去，現在，未来といった時間，地域，天気の内容を聞きとることが大切です。

例題 ニュースを聞き，それに関する質問に対して最も適切なものを選びなさい。 84

1. Why did the executives decide to build the new galleries?

(A) The museum was too small for many of its planned world-class exhibitions.
(B) The museum wasn't highly regarded around the world.
(C) The museum was too old for many of its planned world-class exhibitions.
(D) The museum building was in poor condition. Ⓐ Ⓑ Ⓒ Ⓓ

2. When will the exhibition "Lost Coastal Cultures from Asia to the Mediterranean" take place?

(A) After the new complex is completed
(B) Before the new complex is completed
(C) As soon as 30,000 tickets are sold
(D) It hasn't been decided yet. Ⓐ Ⓑ Ⓒ Ⓓ

もう一度聞いて，下線部に語句を書き入れなさい。

Central Museum is going to become bigger and better. Museum executives have decided the current facility is 1.________________________ many of 2.________________ exhibitions they want to put on and have announced plans to 3.________________. These facilities will house bigger shows and increase the museum's status as one of the best in the world. Unfortunately, however, the new complex 4.________________ in time for September's eagerly 5.______________, "Lost Coastal Cultures from Asia to the Mediterranean," to which the museum has already sold 6.________________.

多くの場合，理由を問う問題に対しての選択肢は文になっています。問 1 のようによく似た文の選択肢の場合，音声の始まる前に文のどこが違うかを少しでも把握しておいたほうがよいでしょう。問 2 のように時間を問う問題はたいてい特定の時間，日にち，期間が短い答えで出ることが多いのですが，副詞節が選択肢になっている場合もあります。このような設問の場合は時に関する叙述に特に注意して聞きとっていきます。音声の後半部分の however，下線 4 の will not ... in time for，下線 6 の前の has already sold などを聞きとります。

Training for the TOEIC L&R Test

PART 4: You will hear two short talks. Select the best answer to each question.

1. According to the weather report, what will the probability of precipitation be in the southern part of the region today?

85

(A) 40%
(B) 50%
(C) 60%
(D) 70%

Ⓐ Ⓑ Ⓒ Ⓓ

2. What will the approximate temperature be this afternoon?

(A) About 17 degrees
(B) About 70 degrees
(C) About 75 degrees
(D) About 80 degrees

Ⓐ Ⓑ Ⓒ Ⓓ

3. Look at the graphic. In which district will the weather change most drastically next Monday?

(A) North
(B) East
(C) West
(D) South

Weekend Weather

	Friday	Saturday	Sunday
North			
East			
West			
South			

Ⓐ Ⓑ Ⓒ Ⓓ

---

4. Look at the graphic. Which level have most of the participating countries agreed on as a CO_2 reduction target?

86

(A) Level 4
(B) Level 3
(C) Level 2
(D) Level 1

CO2 Reduction Target

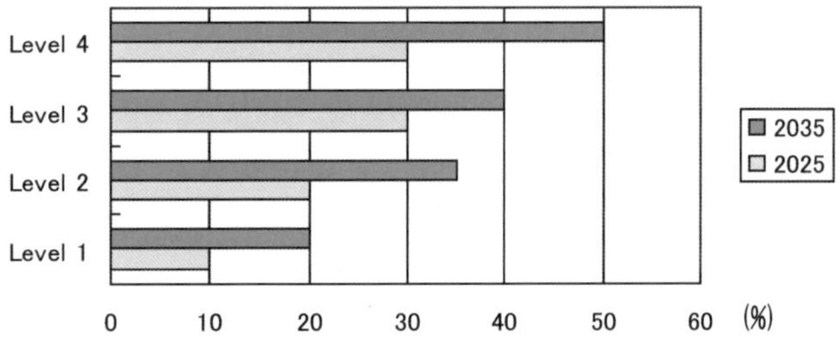

Ⓐ Ⓑ Ⓒ Ⓓ

5. Why has Kingsland been criticized?

(A) It has agreed to a 20% cut in CO_2 emissions.
(B) It has rejected a 20% cut in CO_2 emissions.
(C) It is fighting a war against global warming.
(D) It is responsible for global warming. Ⓐ Ⓑ Ⓒ Ⓓ

6. What has Kingsland's Prime Minister done to cut CO_2 emissions?

(A) Nothing so far
(B) Raised the price of gasoline
(C) Taken part in volunteer activities
(D) Set goals for reducing road-transport emissions Ⓐ Ⓑ Ⓒ Ⓓ

Partial Dictation

Questions 1-3

Good morning. I'm Stephen Stone with the WXZY weather report. According to our 1.______________________________, clouds are spreading over the 2.____________________ of the region, generating 3.________________, with the overall chance of rain standing at 4.__________. Elsewhere in the district, 5.____________________. Sunny skies 6.____________ in the north thanks to warm, dry, 7.________________. Afternoon temperatures will be in the mid-seventies. 8.____________________ will continue through this weekend, but we can expect heavy rain and thunderstorms over the entire district next Monday.

Questions 4-6

The international conference to prevent 1.________________ is being held in Meli. With the exception of Kingsland, most of the participating countries on both sides of the Pacific Ocean have agreed to cut CO_2 emissions 2.______________ by 2025, and by 40% by 2030. Kingsland, which is in target level 1, 3.____________ by criticism charging that it should accept at least a 20% cut in CO_2 emissions by 2025 because it is doing 4.________________ against global warming. But Kingsland Prime Minister Mike Abbott favors 5.______________, sector-by-sector 6.__________, and has set a goal for 7.____________________ road-transport emissions, something that the other nations 8.______________________ upon.

Reading Section　PART 6 気をつけたい助動詞の用法

Technical Point

● まぎらわしい助動詞の意味と使い方を覚える

例題（　　）の中から正しい形を選びなさい。

a) It is not surprising that she (should / would) be good at typing.

b) I suggested that he (look / looks) for a permanent job.

c) You (might as well / might well) feel unhappy to hear such bad news.

d) She (used to / is used to) live in a big city.

e) She (used to / is used to) living in a big city.

f) The door (will not / cannot) open.

a) 感情, 判断を表す形容詞 (または名詞) に続く that 節の中では should が使われます。「It is + 感情・判断を表す形容詞（または名詞）+ that + S + should + 動詞原形」となります。

b) 提案・要求・主張などを表す動詞に続く that 節の中でも should が使われ「S + 提案・命令・主張の V + that + S + should + 動詞原形」となります。
*a), b) のような should はアメリカ英語ではふつう省略し, 動詞の原型を用います (Unit 18 参照)。

c)「～するのはもっともだ」という意味の語句が入ります。

d)「～したものだった」という意味の語句が入ります。would も同じ意味で使われますが，この場合 would は代用できません。would は過去の習慣的動作を表します。「ここはもとは（公園）だった」というような過去の状態を表す時には used to を使います。

e)「～するのに慣れている」という意味の語句が入ります。
*d) の to は不定詞，e) の to は前置詞です。前置詞の後の動詞は V-ing です。

f) は「どうしても～しようとしない」という意味の助動詞が入ります。

[Quiz]（　　）の中から正しい形を選びなさい。

(1) It is a pity that he (should / must) not have won the tournament.

(2) It is requested that no student (leaves / leave) the room till the end of the examination.

(3) This park (would / used to) be a military base years ago.

● 文選択問題は最後に解く

PART 6 の 4 つの空所補充問題のうち，1 問目が「文選択問題」のこともあります。その場合は空所の前，つまりタイトルや宛名などにもヒントがありますので，意識しておきましょう。また，文頭の空所をすぐに埋めようとして選択肢から選ぶより，全体を読んでから判断した方が，文脈に矛盾しない正解文を選ぶことにつながります。他の空所を補充しながら全体を読み，文選択問題は最後に解くようにしましょう。

PART 6: Select the best answers to complete the text.
Questions 1-4 refer to the following announcement.

Thank You

------- (1.) When our company began in 1937, the founders never dreamed that it ------- (2.) grow to become one of the largest insurances and financial services companies in the nation. In the 1940s and early 50s, Star Insurance provided vehicle owners with security and protection like every other auto insurance company. But in 1955, Jack Hampson became CEO and insisted that Star Insurance ------- (3.) ways to distinguish it from its competitors.

More growth and expansion in the 1960s brought about the formation of the Star Insurance Group. Now we ------- (4.) take this opportunity to thank all of the employees, agency staff, and customers who have made our success possible.

Star Insurance Group
70 years serving the nation

1. (A) Star Insurance Group will be moving to a new and larger location next month.
(B) Star Insurance Group is saddened to announce the departure of Jack Hampson.
(C) Star Insurance Group is celebrating its 70th Anniversary.
(D) On behalf of Star Insurance Group, Jack Hampson would like to issue you a formal apology.

Ⓐ Ⓑ Ⓒ Ⓓ

2. (A) will
(B) would
(C) shall
(D) should

Ⓐ Ⓑ Ⓒ Ⓓ

3. (A) find
(B) finds
(C) found
(D) finding

Ⓐ Ⓑ Ⓒ Ⓓ

4. (A) would
(B) used to
(C) would like to
(D) are to

Ⓐ Ⓑ Ⓒ Ⓓ

Reading Section　PART 7 製品などの説明書

Technical Point

●「説明書」は商品の特徴・目的・使い方・注意事項に注意。

説明書では特にその商品の特徴，目的，使い方，注意事項などに注意し，タイトルなどを見て何についての説明文かの予測をつけます。さらに，問題文，答えの選択肢を見てキーワードを把握します。要旨などを問う問題を除いて，問題文は段落順に設問されていることが多いので，問題文を読んで，順番に本文中から答えを検索していきます。速く正確に読み取ることが要求されますが，多少わからない単語があっても読み進めていきます。なお，設問，選択肢は本文中の言葉を言い換えて似た言葉で問うことが多いので注意します。

適切な質問文の例を選んでみましょう。

1) 特徴 ・　　・ a) What is this product for?
2) 警告 ・　　・ b) What is prohibited in regard to this product?
3) 目的 ・　　・ c) How is this product used overseas?
4) 方法 ・　　・ d) Why is this product superior to regular ones?

Training for the TOEIC L&R Test

PART 7: Select the best answer to each question.
Questions 1-3 refer to the following instructions.

In addition to functioning as a regular watch, Happy Time's patented digital DX Watch lets you know precisely how many days, hours, and minutes there are to go before your special future date, such as an anniversary, wedding, university graduation, and so on. To set your DX Watch to your special date, follow these simple steps.

1. Make sure the current time and date are set correctly.
2. Press SD button. The number for the year will start to flash.
3. Press F2 button to advance to your target year. Then press Set button.
4. Notice that the number for the month will be flashing. Press F2 to select your target month. Press Set.
5. Now the number for the date will be flashing. Use F2 to change to your target day and press Set.

The digital display will now show exactly how many days, hours, minutes, and seconds you have until your special future date.

1. What makes this watch different from regular watches?
(A) It tells the correct time.
(B) It serves as an alarm.
(C) It displays the time remaining until a target date.
(D) It helps you achieve your long-term goals.　Ⓐ Ⓑ Ⓒ Ⓓ

2. What does pressing button F2 do?
(A) Advances the time and date
(B) Tells the exact time and date
(C) Sets the target date
(D) Makes it possible to correctly set the current time and date　Ⓐ Ⓑ Ⓒ Ⓓ

3. Which of these is the correct order for setting the target date?
(A) Target year and day, current time and date
(B) Current time and date, target year and day
(C) It varies according to the target day.
(D) There is no specific order.　Ⓐ Ⓑ Ⓒ Ⓓ

Words and Phrases　意味を選んで（　）に記号を書き入れなさい。

U1 Listening Section

1	shelf	(　)	(A) ～で一杯である
2	lie	(　)	(B) 置かれている
3	display	(　)	(C) 買い物客
4	customer	(　)	(D) 掛かる，ぶら下がる
5	dishwasher	(　)	(E) 重ねる
6	stack	(　)	(F) 空の
7	hang	(　)	(G) 掲示物
8	shopper	(　)	(H) 顧客
9	dairy product	(　)	(I) 黒板
10	produce	(　)	(J) 食器洗い機
11	stand	(　)	(K) 設置する
12	empty	(　)	(L) 台
13	arrange	(　)	(M) 棚
14	blackboard	(　)	(N) 陳列
15	be filled with	(　)	(O) 乳製品
16	notice	(　)	(P) 農産物

U1 Reading Section

1	measures	(　)	(A) おつり
2	commission	(　)	(B) 吸収
3	supplier	(　)	(C) 強化された
4	essential	(　)	(D) 許可する
5	permit	(　)	(E) 効果的な
6	fare	(　)	(F) 材料
7	change	(　)	(G) 制裁措置
8	manufacturer	(　)	(H) 代表者
9	reinforced	(　)	(I) 手数料
10	absorption	(　)	(J) 特徴づける
11	feature	(　)	(K) 納入業者
12	ingredient	(　)	(L) 不可欠の
13	representative	(　)	(M) 方策
14	effective	(　)	(N) メーカー
15	sanction	(　)	(O) 憂鬱，不況
16	depression	(　)	(P) 料金，運賃

U2 Listening Section

1	remember	(　)	(A)（人を）車に乗せる
2	last	(　)	(B) 一番最近
3	actually	(　)	(C) 受け入れる
4	give ~ a lift	(　)	(D) 売り上げ
5	lift up	(　)	(E) 売り切れた
6	available	(　)	(F) 覚えている
7	line	(　)	(G) 完成させる
8	sold out	(　)	(H) 行列
9	rack	(　)	(I) 購入する
10	presentation	(　)	(J) 実は
11	baggage	(　)	(K) 昇進
12	manage	(　)	(L) 職，勤め口
13	put on	(　)	(M) 棚
14	complete	(　)	(N) 何とかやっていく
15	accept	(　)	(O) 荷物
16	position	(　)	(P) 入手できる
17	sales	(　)	(Q) 発表
18	promotion	(　)	(R) 身に着ける
19	purchase	(　)	(S) 持ち上げる

U2 Reading Section

1	spinal	(　)	(A) 委員会
2	surgeon	(　)	(B) 開発する
3	develop	(　)	(C) 過酷な
4	inflatable	(　)	(D) 外科医
5	struggle	(　)	(E) しまい込む
6	sit up	(　)	(F) 準拠した
7	patented	(　)	(G) 上体を起こす
8	stow	(　)	(H) 脊椎専門の
9	deck	(　)	(I) 専門家
10	stain	(　)	(J) 適切な
11	harsh	(　)	(K) 投資，買い物
12	the elements	(　)	(L) 特許を取った
13	retailer	(　)	(M) 努力する
14	investment	(　)	(N) 販売店
15	appropriate	(　)	(O) 風雨
16	aligned	(　)	(P) 膨らませることができる
17	board	(　)	(Q) 申込用紙
18	expert	(　)	(R) 木材塗料
19	application form	(　)	(S) 木製テラス

Words and Phrases　意味を選んで（　）に記号を書き入れなさい。

U3 Listening Section

1 employer	（　）	(A) ～に応募する
2 employee	（　）	(B) ～に取り組む
3 salesperson	（　）	(C) ありそうな
4 customer	（　）	(D) 依頼人
5 apply for	（　）	(E) かなり
6 repairperson	（　）	(F) 関係
7 personality	（　）	(G) 感謝する
8 attitude	（　）	(H) 顧客
9 probable	（　）	(I) 締め切り
10 relationship	（　）	(J) 従業員
11 lawyer	（　）	(K) 修理人
12 client	（　）	(L) ストレスを感じる
13 colleague	（　）	(M) 性格
14 deadline	（　）	(N) 態度，心構え
15 feel stressed out	（　）	(O) 同僚
16 field	（　）	(P) 販売員
17 pretty	（　）	(Q) 分野
18 appreciate	（　）	(R) 弁護士
19 work on	（　）	(S) 雇い主

U3 Reading Section

1 figure	（　）	(A) （荷物などを）降ろす
2 Middle Ages	（　）	(B) 会計
3 preserve	（　）	(C) 固い，確固たる
4 management	（　）	(D) 経営陣
5 firm	（　）	(E) 決断，決意
6 decision	（　）	(F) 嫌悪する
7 audience	（　）	(G) 言語学
8 ovation	（　）	(H) 失業中の
9 linguistics	（　）	(I) 数字
10 accounting	（　）	(J) 大喝采
11 distribute	（　）	(K) 耐える
12 indication	（　）	(L) 中世
13 baggage	（　）	(M) 兆候，きざし
14 unload	（　）	(N) 聴衆
15 unemployed	（　）	(O) 手荷物
16 tolerate	（　）	(P) 配布する
17 despise	（　）	(Q) 保存する

U4 Listening Section

1 brave	（　）	(A) 思いやりのある
2 jealous	（　）	(B) 学部長
3 patient	（　）	(C) がっかりした
4 considerate	（　）	(D) 我慢強い
5 secretary	（　）	(E) 緊急の
6 determined	（　）	(F) 詳しい計画
7 discouraged	（　）	(G) 決意を固めた
8 dependable	（　）	(H) 建築家
9 demanding	（　）	(I) 実行する
10 organization	（　）	(J) 嫉妬深い
11 introduce	（　）	(K) 手段
12 attendee	（　）	(L) 出席者
13 physician	（　）	(M) 紹介する
14 architect	（　）	(N) 称賛された
15 dean	（　）	(O) 組織
16 appointment	（　）	(P) 頼りになる
17 blueprint	（　）	(Q) 特権
18 implement	（　）	(R) 内科医
19 resources	（　）	(S) 秘書
20 privilege	（　）	(T) 約束
21 admired	（　）	(U) 勇敢な
22 pressing	（　）	(V) 要求の強い

U4 Reading Section

1 district	（　）	(A) 争い
2 submit	（　）	(B) 入口
3 convince	（　）	(C) 会場
4 approve	（　）	(D) 学問の分野
5 pay back	（　）	(E) 規範から逸脱している
6 principle	（　）	(F) 現象
7 analysis	（　）	(G) 原理
8 survey	（　）	(H) 参加
9 discipline	（　）	(I) 識見
10 empirical	（　）	(J) 実証的な
11 insight	（　）	(K) 主要な
12 phenomena	（　）	(L) 承認する
13 conflict	（　）	(M) 人類学
14 deviant	（　）	(N) 説得する
15 primary	（　）	(O) 地域
16 participation	（　）	(P) 調査
17 anthropology	（　）	(Q) 提出する
18 venue	（　）	(R) 分析
19 entrance	（　）	(S) 返済する
20 text	（　）	(T) メールを送る

Words and Phrases　意味を選んで（　）に記号を書き入れなさい。

U5 Listening Section

1 briefcase	(　)	(A) ～の前に
2 row	(　)	(B) 一列になって
3 wear	(　)	(C) 漕ぐ
4 eyewear	(　)	(D) 芝生
5 put on	(　)	(E) 修理する
6 in line	(　)	(F) 書類かばん
7 in front of	(　)	(G) 注ぐ
8 fix	(　)	(H) 保護ゴーグル
9 glasses	(　)	(I) 身に着けている
10 grass	(　)	(J) 身に着ける
11 pour	(　)	(K) メガネ
12 lean	(　)	(L) もたれる

U5 Reading Section

1 field trip	(　)	(A)（損害などを）被る
2 rush to	(　)	(B)（大規模な）会議
3 manager	(　)	(C) ～に電話する
4 contract	(　)	(D) 急いで行く
5 condition	(　)	(E) 確認する
6 conference	(　)	(F) 課長
7 observation tower	(　)	(G) 携帯電話
8 shipment	(　)	(H) 契約
9 give ~ a ring	(　)	(I) 校外学習
10 cell phone	(　)	(J) 条件
11 material	(　)	(K) 資料，材料
12 confirm	(　)	(L) 損害，痛手
13 suffer	(　)	(M) 展望塔
14 loss	(　)	(N) 発送，発送品

U6 Listening Section

1 business trip	(　)	(A) ～へ出発する
2 temperature	(　)	(B) 市場
3 degree	(　)	(C) 角，隅
4 Celsius	(　)	(D) 気温，温度
5 increase	(　)	(E) 出張
6 product	(　)	(F) 製品
7 leave for	(　)	(G) セ氏
8 fastest	(　)	(H) 増加させる
9 bean	(　)	(I) 度
10 corner	(　)	(J) 文房具
11 market	(　)	(K) 豆
12 stationery	(　)	(L) 最も速い

U6 Reading Section

1 annual	(　)	(A)（事業）計画
2 excerpt	(　)	(B) ～の大部分
3 scheme	(　)	(C) もはや～ない
4 reimburse	(　)	(D) 影響する
5 affect	(　)	(E) 回覧する
6 criteria	(　)	(F) 勧める
7 the bulk of ~	(　)	(G) 基準
8 claimant	(　)	(H) 四半期
9 recommend	(　)	(I) 承認する
10 approve	(　)	(J) 請求者
11 set out	(　)	(K) 日時が重なること
12 quarter	(　)	(L) 年1回の
13 reflect	(　)	(M) 発表する
14 circulate	(　)	(N) 抜粋
15 no longer ~	(　)	(O) 反映する
16 clash	(　)	(P) 返済する

Words and Phrases　意味を選んで（　）に記号を書き入れなさい。

U7 Listening Section

1 main character	(　　)	(A) ～を世話する
2 respect	(　　)	(B) 鑑賞する
3 boring	(　　)	(C) 計算する，計る
4 inspire	(　　)	(D) 断る
5 especially	(　　)	(E) 鼓舞する
6 exhibition	(　　)	(F) 主人公
7 admission	(　　)	(G) 出席する
8 fee	(　　)	(H) 小旅行
9 interactive	(　　)	(I) 双方向の
10 display	(　　)	(J) 尊敬する
11 calculate	(　　)	(K) つまらない
12 take care of	(　　)	(L) 展示会
13 turn down	(　　)	(M) 特に
14 appreciate	(　　)	(N) 入場
15 allot	(　　)	(O) 述べる，話す
16 excursion	(　　)	(P) 表示，展示
17 attend	(　　)	(Q) 料金
18 mention	(　　)	(R) 割り振る

U7 Reading Section

1 accurately	(　　)	(A) （勘定書で）請求する
2 neat	(　　)	(B) ～に関して
3 previous	(　　)	(C) きちんとした
4 copier	(　　)	(D) 検索する
5 eyesight	(　　)	(E) 効率的な
6 vice-president	(　　)	(F) 誤植
7 obtain	(　　)	(G) コピー機
8 sales quota	(　　)	(H) 視力
9 delivery	(　　)	(I) 正確に
10 bill	(　　)	(J) 通勤（通学）する
11 typographical error	(　　)	(K) 手に入れる
12 commute	(　　)	(L) 配達
13 retrieve	(　　)	(M) 販売ノルマ
14 efficient	(　　)	(N) 副社長
15 document	(　　)	(O) 文書，書類
16 regarding	(　　)	(P) 前の

U8 Listening Section

1 résumé	(　　)	(A) 一流の
2 internship	(　　)	(B) 改修工事
3 impressive	(　　)	(C) 確定する
4 in person	(　　)	(D) 感銘を与える
5 details	(　　)	(E) 現在のところ
6 overbook	(　　)	(F) 研修
7 budget	(　　)	(G) 最新情報
8 currently	(　　)	(H) 最先端
9 renovation	(　　)	(I) 施設
10 available	(　　)	(J) 実験室
11 laboratory	(　　)	(K) 宿泊施設
12 equipment	(　　)	(L) 詳細
13 institution	(　　)	(M) 創造
14 astronomy	(　　)	(N) 装置
15 physics	(　　)	(O) 代行の，それに代わる
16 inquiry	(　　)	(P) 調査
17 update	(　　)	(Q) 直接，じかに
18 alternative	(　　)	(R) 定員以上の予約を受ける
19 accommodations	(　　)	(S) 天文学
20 finalize	(　　)	(T) 並外れた
21 extraordinary	(　　)	(U) 物理学
22 creativity	(　　)	(V) 文化人類学
23 anthropology	(　　)	(W) 予算
24 leading	(　　)	(X) 利用できる
25 forefront	(　　)	(Y) 履歴書

U8 Reading Section

1 frankness	(　　)	(A) ～する限り
2 qualified	(　　)	(B) ～と言い表される
3 contribution	(　　)	(C) ～と混同される
4 insofar	(　　)	(D) ～と間違われる
5 negligence	(　　)	(E) 胃
6 at the last minute	(　　)	(F) 一般に
7 departure date	(　　)	(G) 医療検査
8 draw	(　　)	(H) 価格に敏感な
9 typically	(　　)	(I) 過失，不注意
10 be eager to	(　　)	(J) 貢献
11 otherwise	(　　)	(K) さもなければ
12 price-sensitive	(　　)	(L) 資格のある
13 heart attack	(　　)	(M) しきりに～したがる
14 heartburn	(　　)	(N) 出発日
15 estimate	(　　)	(O) 症状
16 last	(　　)	(P) 心臓発作
17 be described as	(　　)	(Q) 推定する
18 stomach	(　　)	(R) 素直さ
19 throat	(　　)	(S) 近づく
20 perception	(　　)	(T) 直前に
21 symptom	(　　)	(U) 続く
22 be confused with	(　　)	(V) 認識
23 be mistaken for	(　　)	(W) 喉
24 medical evaluation	(　　)	(X) はっきりと
25 definitely	(　　)	(Y) 胸やけ

Words and Phrases　意味を選んで（　）に記号を書き入れなさい。

U9 Listening Section

1 under	(　)	(A)	(行為などが)進行中で
2 grow	(　)	(B)	～しようとしている
3 parking lot	(　)	(C)	～につながる
4 be about to	(　)	(D)	～に向き合う
5 passenger	(　)	(E)	～まで
6 board	(　)	(F)	オープンカー
7 pedestrian	(　)	(G)	屋上,(自動車の)幌
8 steps	(　)	(H)	降りている，下にある
9 lead	(　)	(I)	階段
10 up to	(　)	(J)	乗客
11 wave	(　)	(K)	育つ
12 top	(　)	(L)	たなびく,手を振る
13 palm tree	(　)	(M)	駐車場
14 convertible	(　)	(N)	乗り込む,搭乗する
15 face	(　)	(O)	歩行者
16 down	(　)	(P)	ヤシの木

U9 Reading Section

1 anyway	(　)	(A)	～に影響する
2 review	(　)	(B)	～を考慮に入れる
3 draft	(　)	(C)	宴会
4 paper	(　)	(D)	家具付きの
5 reception	(　)	(E)	企業
6 approve	(　)	(F)	原稿，草稿
7 oppose	(　)	(G)	賛成する
8 colleague	(　)	(H)	指示
9 warranty	(　)	(I)	同僚
10 take ~ into account	(　)	(J)	とにかく
11 instruction	(　)	(K)	取り組み，行為
12 furnished	(　)	(L)	反対する
13 real estate	(　)	(M)	不動産
14 corporation	(　)	(N)	保証
15 practice	(　)	(O)	見直す
16 affect	(　)	(P)	論文

U10 Listening Section

1 production	(　)	(A)	～と見なす
2 manager	(　)	(B)	おそらく
3 document	(　)	(C)	収集する
4 nearly	(　)	(D)	修正する
5 probably	(　)	(E)	書類
6 wrong	(　)	(F)	生産
7 direction	(　)	(G)	入力
8 correct	(　)	(H)	部長，課長
9 entry	(　)	(I)	方向
10 error	(　)	(J)	ほとんど～である
11 collect	(　)	(K)	間違い
12 consider	(　)	(L)	間違った

U10 Reading Section

1 hit upon	(　)	(A)	～の申請をする
2 disturb	(　)	(B)	～を思いつく
3 instruction permit	(　)	(C)	受付
4 vehicle	(　)	(D)	運用能力
5 apply for	(　)	(E)	応募者
6 renewal	(　)	(F)	外資系の
7 progress	(　)	(G)	仮免許
8 valid	(　)	(H)	現在の
9 state	(　)	(I)	更新
10 licensed	(　)	(J)	顧客
11 pharmaceutical company	(　)	(K)	邪魔をする
12 receptionist	(　)	(L)	州
13 candidate	(　)	(M)	進歩
14 command	(　)	(N)	製薬会社
15 attachment	(　)	(O)	添付
16 current	(　)	(P)	乗物
17 customer	(　)	(Q)	免許を持っている
18 foreign-affiliated	(　)	(R)	有効な

Words and Phrases　意味を選んで（　）に記号を書き入れなさい。

U11 Listening Section

1	attend	(　)	(A) ～かどうか
2	symptom	(　)	(B) ～に欠けている
3	sore throat	(　)	(C) ～の代わりを務める
4	runny nose	(　)	(D) ～の後任になる
5	bad cough	(　)	(E) 急いで帰る
6	promotion	(　)	(F) 薬
7	sales	(　)	(G) 出席する
8	department	(　)	(H) 症状
9	human resources	(　)	(I) 昇進
10	challenging	(　)	(J) 人事
11	lack	(　)	(K) のどの痛み
12	sit in for	(　)	(L) 鼻水
13	medicine	(　)	(M) 販売
14	run home	(　)	(N) ひどいせき
15	head	(　)	(O) 部（会社の組織）
16	if	(　)	(P) 部長
17	replace	(　)	(Q) やりがいのある

U11 Reading Section

1	close down	(　)	(A) 火薬
2	accident	(　)	(B) けが
3	confuse	(　)	(C) すぐに
4	thrill	(　)	(D) 心を豊かにする
5	hardly	(　)	(E) 混乱させる
6	reportedly	(　)	(F) 事故
7	gunpowder	(　)	(G) 消費者
8	explosive device	(　)	(H) 繊細な
9	fine	(　)	(I) 調査する
10	consumer	(　)	(J) 提案する
11	green tea	(　)	(K) 爆発装置
12	ship	(　)	(L) 閉鎖する
13	enrich	(　)	(M) 報道によると
14	injury	(　)	(N) ほとんど～ない
15	immediately	(　)	(O) 輸送する
16	propose	(　)	(P) 緑茶
17	survey	(　)	(Q) わくわくさせる

U12 Listening Section

1	destination	(　)	(A) ～の代わりに
2	instead of	(　)	(B) ～のために，～が原因で
3	due to	(　)	(C) ～のように見える
4	passenger	(　)	(D) ～を代表して
5	lost	(　)	(E) 位置する
6	gate attendant	(　)	(F) 受付係
7	turbulence	(　)	(G) 動き回る
8	on the way	(　)	(H) 遅らせる
9	on time	(　)	(I) およそ，約
10	delay	(　)	(J) 血縁の，きょうだいの
11	appear to	(　)	(K) 現地時間
12	related	(　)	(L) 時間通りに，予定通りに
13	description	(　)	(M) 自由に ～ する
14	locate	(　)	(N) 乗客
15	on behalf of	(　)	(O) 直行便
16	nonstop service	(　)	(P) 途中で
17	approximately	(　)	(Q) 描写
18	be free to	(　)	(R) 迷子の
19	move about	(　)	(S) 目的地
20	local time	(　)	(T) 乱気流

U12 Reading Section

1	business trip	(　)	(A)（履修）単位
2	assist	(　)	(B) ～だと考える
3	credit	(　)	(C) ～の場合に備えて
4	required	(　)	(D) 改良する
5	syllabus	(　)	(E) 感謝する
6	stop by	(　)	(F) 居住者
7	enclose	(　)	(G) 緊急の
8	absence	(　)	(H) 欠席
9	water outage	(　)	(I) 講義概要
10	emergency	(　)	(J) 工事請負人，業者
11	plumbing	(　)	(K) 妨げる
12	contractor	(　)	(L) 出張
13	deem	(　)	(M) 助ける
14	leak	(　)	(N) 立ち寄る
15	in case	(　)	(O) 断水
16	issue	(　)	(P) 同封する
17	appreciate	(　)	(Q) 配管設備
18	contact	(　)	(R) 必修の
19	resident	(　)	(S) 問題
20	upgrade	(　)	(T) 連絡を取る
21	interrupt	(　)	(U) 漏水

Words and Phrases　意味を選んで（　）に記号を書き入れなさい。

U13 Listening Section

1 shake hands	(　　)	(A)（街頭の）物売り
2 around	(　　)	(B)（交通が）激しい
3 side by side	(　　)	(C) ～に乗る，～に間に合う
4 catch	(　　)	(D) ～の周りに
5 sweep	(　　)	(E) ～を見る
6 heavy	(　　)	(F) 握手をする
7 sidewalk	(　　)	(G) 一斉に沸き起こる
8 vender	(　　)	(H) 柵
9 merchandise	(　　)	(I) 出演者
10 look at	(　　)	(J) 商品
11 fence	(　　)	(K) 聴衆
12 sunbathe	(　　)	(L) 日光浴をする
13 audience	(　　)	(M) 掃く
14 performer	(　　)	(N) 歩道
15 a round of	(　　)	(O) 横に並んで

U13 Reading Section

1 lie	(　　)	(A) お金などを貸す
2 lay	(　　)	(B) 借りる
3 borrow	(　　)	(C) 気温
4 rent	(　　)	(D) 協力，共同制作
5 lend	(　　)	(E) 候補者
6 collaboration	(　　)	(F) 最高経営責任者
7 examination table	(　　)	(G) 書類
8 document	(　　)	(H) 診察台
9 temperature	(　　)	(I) 設立する
10 election	(　　)	(J) 選挙
11 governor	(　　)	(K) 知事
12 candidate	(　　)	(L) 申込書
13 application form	(　　)	(M) 有料で借りる，貸す
14 chief executive officer	(　　)	(N) 横に置く，横たえる
15 found	(　　)	(O) 横になる

U14 Listening Section

1 on average	(　　)	(A)（時間など）を必要とする
2 forum	(　　)	(B)（病気など）にかかる
3 have never been to	(　　)	(C)（物事が）始まる
4 most of	(　　)	(D) ～してはいかがですか
5 catch	(　　)	(E) ～に行ったことがない
6 flu	(　　)	(F) ～の間
7 attend	(　　)	(G) インフルエンザ
8 Why don't you ~?	(　　)	(H) 公開討論会
9 take	(　　)	(I) 出席する，参加する
10 at least	(　　)	(J) 少なくとも
11 get underway	(　　)	(K) 手伝い，助手
12 hire	(　　)	(L) 平均して
13 assistant	(　　)	(M) ほとんどの
14 during	(　　)	(N) 雇う

U14 Reading Section

1 client	(　　)	(A) 医学博士
2 insurance	(　　)	(B) 依頼人，顧客
3 pediatrics	(　　)	(C) 患者
4 practice	(　　)	(D) 器具，台所用品
5 biology	(　　)	(E) 研修（期間）
6 internship	(　　)	(F) 幸運な
7 patient	(　　)	(G) 材料，食材
8 fortunate	(　　)	(H) 蒸気の抜け穴，通気口
9 MD	(　　)	(I) 小児科
10 ingredient	(　　)	(J) 初心者
11 novice	(　　)	(K) 診療所
12 utensil	(　　)	(L) 生物学
13 withstand	(　　)	(M) 耐える
14 lid	(　　)	(N) 融ける
15 vent	(　　)	(O) 残っている
16 burst	(　　)	(P) 破裂する
17 melt	(　　)	(Q) ふた
18 remaining	(　　)	(R) 保険

Words and Phrases　意味を選んで（　）に記号を書き入れなさい。

U15 Listening Section

1	go with	(　)	(A)	営業部長
2	loud	(　)	(B)	角
3	round	(　)	(C)	掲示
4	tip	(　)	(D)	契約（書）
5	reserve	(　)	(E)	交渉する
6	rooftop	(　)	(F)	材料
7	contract	(　)	(G)	先端
8	material	(　)	(H)	調和する，～と合う
9	briefing	(　)	(I)	派手な
10	promotional	(　)	(J)	販売促進の
11	notice	(　)	(K)	丸い
12	corner	(　)	(L)	向かい側の
13	opposite	(　)	(M)	もちろん（強い肯定）
14	sales manager	(　)	(N)	屋根
15	negotiate	(　)	(O)	予定を組みなおす
16	reschedule	(　)	(P)	予約する
17	definitely	(　)	(Q)	連絡会議

U15 Reading Section

1	come by	(　)	(A)	～に…することを強いる
2	provide	(　)	(B)	を承認する
3	efficiency	(　)	(C)	～を取り扱う
4	force	(　)	(D)	～を納得させる
5	conscious	(　)	(E)	～を理解させる
6	Business Administration	(　)	(F)	意識的な
7	timber	(　)	(G)	合併する
8	fall	(　)	(H)	企業経営学
9	merge	(　)	(I)	下落する
10	comprehend	(　)	(J)	研究所
11	satisfaction	(　)	(K)	効率
12	empirical	(　)	(L)	実証的な
13	convince	(　)	(M)	立ち寄る
14	council	(　)	(N)	提供する
15	approve	(　)	(O)	評議会
16	laboratory	(　)	(P)	満足
17	treat	(　)	(Q)	木材

U16 Listening Section

1	tour	(　)	(A)	（範囲などを）扱う
2	double-decker	(　)	(B)	～から成り立っている
3	be steeped in	(　)	(C)	～で満ちている
4	explore	(　)	(D)	～を見て回る
5	rowing	(　)	(E)	2階建ての
6	introductory	(　)	(F)	AをBとしてとらえる
7	geography	(　)	(G)	BからAを取りそろえる
8	brief	(　)	(H)	概要を示す
9	consist of	(　)	(I)	期間
10	outline	(　)	(J)	重要性，価値
11	draw A from B	(　)	(K)	宿泊施設，宿泊費用
12	cover	(　)	(L)	達成する
13	duration	(　)	(M)	地理
14	achieve	(　)	(N)	問い合わせ
15	enquiry	(　)	(O)	入門用の
16	accommodation	(　)	(P)	ボートレースの
17	attraction	(　)	(Q)	魅力
18	charm	(　)	(R)	催し物
19	take A as B	(　)	(S)	要点を伝える
20	significance	(　)	(T)	旅行する

U16 Reading Section

1	regarding	(　)	(A)	～経由で
2	especially	(　)	(B)	～に関する
3	aspect	(　)	(C)	～までに，～より遅くならずに
4	individual	(　)	(D)	～を与える，供給する
5	peer	(　)	(E)	～を示す，表に出す
6	demonstrate	(　)	(F)	～を促進する，強く進める
7	reflect on	(　)	(G)	～を提出する
8	personal	(　)	(H)	～をよく考える
9	attribute	(　)	(I)	個々の，個人
10	terrific	(　)	(J)	個人的な
11	decline	(　)	(K)	個人的に
12	audit	(　)	(L)	断る
13	encourage	(　)	(M)	事前に
14	provide	(　)	(N)	素晴らしい
15	in advance	(　)	(O)	聴講する，監査する
16	submit	(　)	(P)	特質，側面
17	via	(　)	(Q)	特性，属性
18	no later than	(　)	(R)	特に，際立って
19	in person	(　)	(S)	仲間，クラスメート

Words and Phrases　意味を選んで（　）に記号を書き入れなさい。

U17 Listening Section

1	climb	(　)	(A) ～のそばに
2	cash register	(　)	(B) ～を横切って，越えて
3	stack	(　)	(C) アスファルト
4	shelf	(　)	(D) 線路
5	across	(　)	(E) 棚
6	bush	(　)	(F) 積み上げる
7	beside	(　)	(G) 低木
8	track	(　)	(H) 荷物を積む
9	pave	(　)	(I) 登る
10	asphalt	(　)	(J) はしご
11	ladder	(　)	(K) 舗装する
12	load	(　)	(L) レジ
13	station wagon	(　)	(M) ワゴン車

U17 Reading Section

1	contract	(　)	(A) ～を避ける
2	invest	(　)	(B) 幹部，高官
3	bond	(　)	(C) 契約
4	updated	(　)	(D) 現在の
5	current	(　)	(E) 債権
6	investigate	(　)	(F) 最新の
7	avoid	(　)	(G) 洗練された
8	offer	(　)	(H) 調査する
9	ship	(　)	(I) 統計
10	presentation	(　)	(J) 投資する
11	polished	(　)	(K) 発送する
12	executive	(　)	(L) 発表
13	analysis	(　)	(M) 分析
14	statistics	(　)	(N) 申し出

U18 Listening Section

1	sales clerk	(　)	(A) (問題などが)発生する
2	plant	(　)	(B) ～することになっている
3	manager	(　)	(C) ～まで
4	contact	(　)	(D) ～を考慮に入れる
5	contract	(　)	(E) 緊急の，差し迫った
6	be supposed to	(　)	(F) 契約書
7	urgent	(　)	(G) 口座
8	come up	(　)	(H) 工場，設備
9	already	(　)	(I) すでに，もう
10	account	(　)	(J) ただちに
11	take ~ into account	(　)	(K) 店員，販売員
12	until	(　)	(L) 部長，責任者
13	right away	(　)	(M) 連絡を取る

U18 Reading Section

1	opportunity	(　)	(A) ～につき
2	fit in	(　)	(B) ～に慣れる
3	CV	(　)	(C) とけ込む
4	applicant	(　)	(D) 応募者
5	seasoned	(　)	(E) 機会
6	portfolio	(　)	(F) 経験豊かな
7	diverse	(　)	(G) 工芸品
8	get used to ~	(　)	(H) 作品集
9	culinary	(　)	(I) 参加登録する
10	stimulating	(　)	(J) 刺激的な
11	craft	(　)	(K) 多様な
12	enquiry	(　)	(L) 適する
13	cuisine	(　)	(M) 問い合わせ
14	per	(　)	(N) 履歴書
15	suit	(　)	(O) 料理
16	sign up	(　)	(P) 料理の

Words and Phrases　意味を選んで（　）に記号を書き入れなさい。

U19 Listening Section

1 deal	(　)	(A) ～に失敗する
2 postpone	(　)	(B) ～を実行する
3 work out	(　)	(C) ～を進出させる，始める
4 negotiate	(　)	(D) ～を達成する
5 warehouse	(　)	(E) AだけでなくBも
6 product	(　)	(F) うまくいかない
7 launch	(　)	(G) 延期する
8 competitor	(　)	(H) 競争相手
9 domestic	(　)	(I) 効果的に
10 customer	(　)	(J) 交渉する
11 attract	(　)	(K) 顧客
12 meet	(　)	(L) 国内の
13 sales quota	(　)	(M) 最新の
14 investor	(　)	(N) 製品
15 go wrong	(　)	(O) 倉庫
16 implement	(　)	(P) 投資家
17 latest	(　)	(Q) 取引
18 not only A but B	(　)	(R) 販売ノルマ
19 fail to	(　)	(S) 引きつける
20 effectively	(　)	(T) 良い結果となる

U19 Reading Section

1 land	(　)	(A)（企業の）合併吸収
2 convention	(　)	(B)（目的に）合う
3 rest	(　)	(C) ～に当てはまる
4 growth rate	(　)	(D) ～を承認する
5 convince	(　)	(E) ～を説得する
6 approve	(　)	(F) アレルギー
7 be true of	(　)	(G) 管理者，上司
8 distribute	(　)	(H) 休息
9 supplier	(　)	(I) 講習会
10 deliver	(　)	(J) 実演説明
11 workshop	(　)	(K) すべて予約する
12 protection	(　)	(L) 成長率
13 M&A	(　)	(M) 大会，会議
14 supervisor	(　)	(N) 着陸する，上陸する
15 demonstration	(　)	(O) 納入業者
16 allergy	(　)	(P) 配達する
17 fit	(　)	(Q) 配布する，割り当てる
18 book up	(　)	(R) 保護，防衛策

U20 Listening Section

1 exhibition	(　)	(A) ～に対して責任がある
2 complex	(　)	(B) ～を生み出す，～を起こす
3 facility	(　)	(C) およその，約～
4 house	(　)	(D) 気温
5 status	(　)	(E) 拒否する
6 region	(　)	(F) 削減
7 approximate	(　)	(G) 産業別の
8 temperature	(　)	(H) 収容する
9 reduction	(　)	(I) 首相
10 criticize	(　)	(J) 主要な
11 emission	(　)	(K) 設備，施設
12 reject	(　)	(L) 責める，とがめる
13 global warming	(　)	(M) 全体の
14 be responsible for	(　)	(N) 地位
15 Prime Minister	(　)	(O) 地域
16 spread	(　)	(P) 地球温暖化
17 generate	(　)	(Q) 展示品
18 mid	(　)	(R) 半ば
19 thunderstorm	(　)	(S) 排出，排出量
20 entire	(　)	(T) 激しい雷雨
21 leading	(　)	(U) 非難する
22 sector-by-sector	(　)	(V) 広がる
23 charge	(　)	(W) 複合施設

U20 Reading Section

1 permanent	(　)	(A) ～と…を区別する
2 military base	(　)	(B) ～を主張する
3 founder	(　)	(C) 祝う
4 insurance	(　)	(D) 海外で
5 financial	(　)	(E) 拡大
6 vehicle	(　)	(F) 機能，機能する
7 insist	(　)	(G) 禁止する
8 distinguish ~ from ...	(　)	(H) 金融の
9 expansion	(　)	(I) 軍の基地
10 formation	(　)	(J) 形態，構造
11 celebrate	(　)	(K) 現在の時間
12 apology	(　)	(L) 常任の，終身の
13 prohibit	(　)	(M) 謝罪
14 overseas	(　)	(N) 進める
15 function	(　)	(O) 正確に
16 patented	(　)	(P) 創設者
17 precisely	(　)	(Q) 特許を持つ
18 current time	(　)	(R) 残りの，残っている
19 advance	(　)	(S) 乗物，車両
20 remaining	(　)	(T) 保険

Effective Approach for the TOEIC®L&R Test <Revised Edition>
TOEIC®L&R テスト：スコアアップのための総合英語［改訂新版］ ［B-915］

1 刷　2021 年 1 月 30 日
3 刷　2023 年 8 月 30 日

著　者	田中　清美	Kiyomi Tanaka
	和田　ゆり	Yuri Wada
	榊　哲	Satoru Sakaki
	金子　麻子	Asako Kaneko

発行者　南雲　一範　Kazunori Nagumo
発行所　株式会社　南雲堂
〒162-0801　東京都新宿区山吹町361
NAN'UN-DO Co., Ltd.
361 Yamabuki-cho, Shinjuku-ku, Tokyo 162-0801, Japan
振替口座：00160-0-46863
TEL:　03-3268-2311（営業部：学校関係）
03-3268-2384（営業部：書店関係）
03-3268-2387（編集部）
FAX:　03-3269-2486
編集者　加藤　敦

組　版　中西　史子

装　丁　Nスタジオ

検　印　省　略

コード　ISBN978-4-523-17915-3　C0082

Printed in Japan

E-mail : nanundo@post.email.ne.jp
URL : https://www.nanun-do.co.jp/